I0129980

Flashy, Fun and Functional

Studies in Australasian Historical Archaeology

Martin Gibbs and Angela Middleton, Series Editors

The Studies in Australasian Historical Archaeology series aims to publish excavation reports and regional syntheses that deal with research into the historical archaeology of Australia, New Zealand and the Asia-Pacific region. The series aims to encourage greater public access to the results of major research and consultancy investigations, and it is co-published with the Australasian Society for Historical Archaeology.

Flashy, Fun and Functional

How Things Helped to Invent Melbourne's Gold Rush Mayor

Sarah Hayes

Studies in Australasian Historical Archaeology
Volume 6

SYDNEY UNIVERSITY PRESS

Published 2018 by Sydney University Press
In association with the Australasian Society for Historical Archaeology
asha.org.au

ASHA
AUSTRALASIAN SOCIETY FOR
HISTORICAL ARCHAEOLOGY

© Sarah Hayes 2018
© Sydney University Press 2018

Reproduction and Communication for Other Purposes
Except as permitted under the Copyright Act, no part of this edition may be reproduced, stored in a retrieval system, or communicated in any form or by any means without prior written permission. All requests for reproduction or communication should be made to Sydney University Press at the address below:

Sydney University Press
Fisher Library F03
University of Sydney NSW 2006
AUSTRALIA
sup.info@sydney.edu.au
sydney.edu.au/sup

NATIONAL
LIBRARY
OF AUSTRALIA

A catalogue record for this book is available from the National Library of Australia.

ISBN 9781743326152 paperback
ISBN 9781743322123 PDF
ISBN 9781743322642 epub

Cover image: Transfer-printed chamber pot (HA1657).

Cover design by Miguel Yamin.

Contents

List of Figures

List of Plates

List of Tables

Abbreviations

ADB	Australian Dictionary of Biography
AOT	Archives Office of Tasmania
BDM	Birth, Deaths and Marriages Records: written in-text as 'BDM Place of Jurisdiction, number with type of record (b = birth, m = marriage, d = death) / year', where Place of Jurisdiction is NSW (New South Wales), QLD (Queensland) or VIC (Victoria)
LUV GLL	Land Use Victoria General Law Library, Laverton
MCC	Melbourne City Council; in Public Record Office Victoria listings MCC records are held under VA 511 Melbourne (Town 1842–1847; City 1847–ct)
NRS	New South Wales Record Series [in State Archives New South Wales listings]
PROV	Public Record Office Victoria
SANSW	State Archives New South Wales
VA	Victorian Agency [in Public Record Office Victoria listings]
VPRS	Victorian Public Record Series [in Public Record Office Victoria listings]

Acknowledgements

This research was conducted as part of an Australian Research Council project – *Suburban Archaeology: Approaching the Archaeology of the Middle Class in 19th Century Melbourne* (DP1093001) – held by La Trobe University, Deakin University and the University of Melbourne. Chief investigators on the project were Tim Murray, Susan Lawrence, Andrew May and Linda Young and I thank them for their input in shaping this research.

My research was conducted at La Trobe University and benefitted from the intellectual and technical support offered by the Department of Archaeology and History. Particular thanks to Ming Wei for preparing figures and typesetting the volume.

Thank you to Charlotte Smith and Museum Victoria for access to the collection, support and use of museum facilities.

A heartfelt thanks to historian Barbara Minchinton who conducted research into the lives of the Smiths for this project, edited this volume and prepared it for publication. Also to Noriaki Sato for his input on the theoretical aspects of this paper.

Introduction

Each time Mayor John Thomas Smith (**Figure 1**) walked through Melbourne in the course of his business he was sure to have with him a 'daily largesse of £5 or £6 in silver ...' which he duly distributed 'amongst the poor and needy' (*Bendigo Advertiser*, 31 January 1879:3). He was a well-known figure, recognisable by his stout build, white top hat, shirt frills and cutty pipe (Eastwood 1976:151). Much criticised in the local paper for his brash ways and underhand dealings, his false ostentation and harsh reaction to the Eureka uprising (*The Argus*, 19 September 1848:2–3, 30 May 1850:4, 5 September 1856:5, 1 May 1857:5; Hocking 2004:154–157), he was nonetheless a successful and benevolent man who supported a number of charities and championed improvements for the working man (*The Argus*, 31 January 1879:6; *Bendigo Advertiser*, 31 January 1879:3).

What makes Smith so interesting to me as a historical archaeologist is the trajectory of his life from his convict parentage to Mayor of Melbourne; specifically, the role that cultural capital played in the family's rapid rise and how this related to Melbourne's changing and diversifying middle class. John Thomas Smith was born in May 1816 to John, a Scottish shoemaker transported around age 18 to 21, and Elizabeth, colonial born daughter of convict parents. He was apprenticed to a builder and joiner in Sydney and might have had indentures as a clerk in his youth. He made the move that would redefine his life in 1837 when he travelled to Melbourne and became an assistant teacher at the Aboriginal Mission Station on the Yarra River. Not long afterwards he married Ellen Pender (**Figure 2**), the daughter of an Irish Catholic publican, and they had five sons and four daughters. His wealth increased after his marriage: he became a hotel owner, then operator of a theatre – the first in Melbourne. His success culminated in his becoming Lord Mayor of Melbourne by 1851 and being re-elected multiple times (Hetherington 1964:92; Eastwood 1976:150–151). He remained a wealthy property owner and businessman from that time on.

Figure 1: John Thomas Smith, 1872 (Creator: Thomas Foster Chuck; Source: State Library of Victoria, www.slv.vic.gov.au).

Figure 2: Ellen Smith (Source: Margaret Torning Foster, descendent).

Smith took every opportunity available to him at this unique time and place in history. Melbourne was a free settlement, commencing officially in 1839, and was proud of it. Yet the unclear backgrounds of migrants in the early years coupled with the fact that those from lowly backgrounds dramatically outnumbered the upper crust created a golden opportunity for social mobility (Cannon 1975:207–208; Swain 2005:668–669). Smith, and his family, are representative of those new Melbournians arriving prior to the gold rush who successfully negotiated their way into the ranks of the middle class and in doing so redefined the nature of society. This was the epitome of the Australian dream – to move beyond the status you were born with.

The Smiths' home at 300 Queen Street, Melbourne, which they occupied from 1849 until 1860 (**Figure 3**), provides an opportunity to explore the use of material culture in their upward social mobility. The Georgian manor comprising eight rooms and four cellars was one of the first town houses in a fashionable residential part of Melbourne (Priestley 1984:26–27) close to Flagstaff Hill (**Figure 4** and **Figure 5**). The home is now an office building with a tower in what was once its backyard. Beneath this tower lie the remains of the Smith family's cesspit. The heritage significance of the site meant that when it was redeveloped as offices in the early 1980s it was subject to an archaeological investigation.

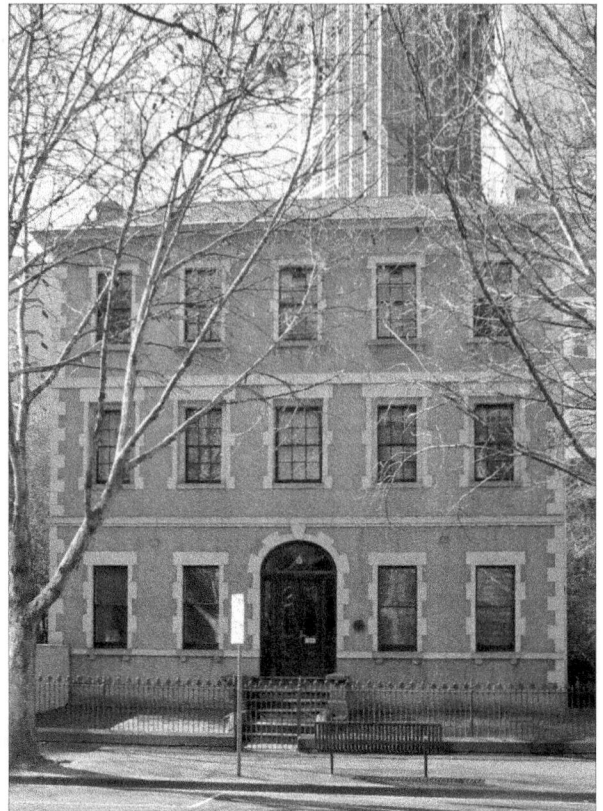

Figure 3: 300 Queen Street, Melbourne (Source: Peter Maltezos).

Figure 4: Location of Melbourne, Victoria also showing Viewbank approximately 25 kilometres north-east of the city (Source: Ming Wei).

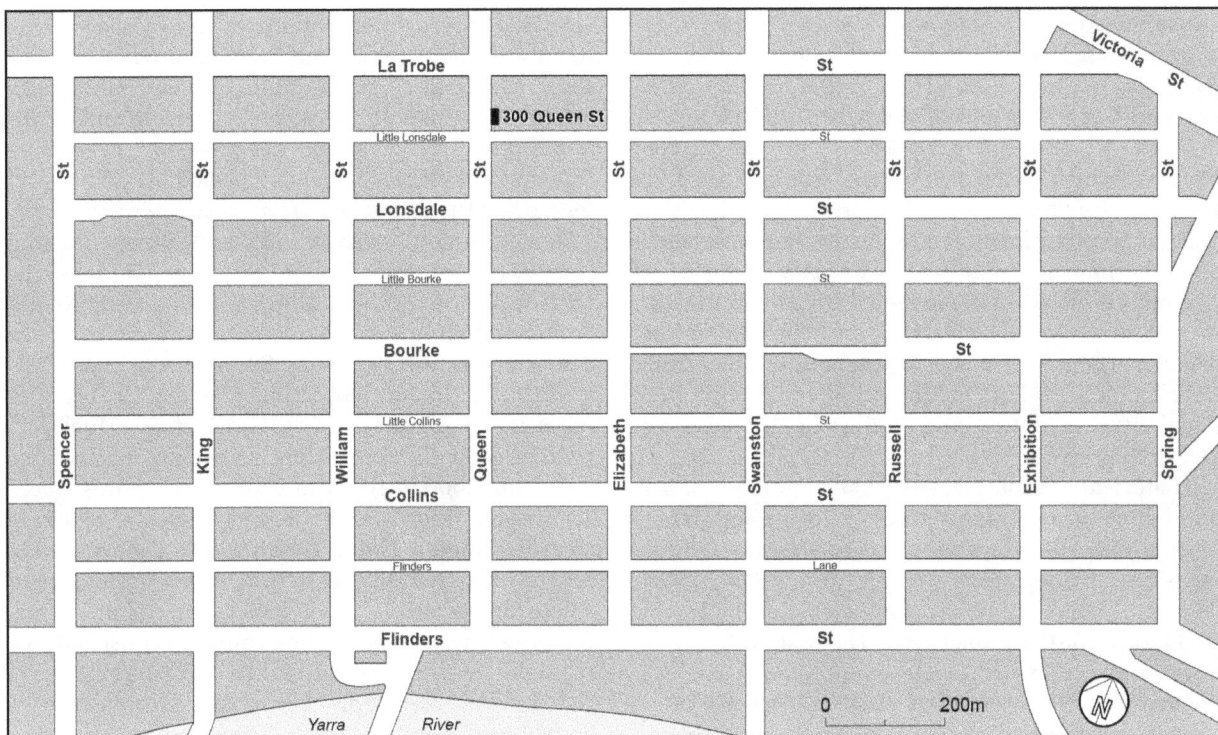

Figure 5: Location of 300 Queen Street within Melbourne's CBD (Source: Ming Wei).

One of the earliest urban excavations in Australia, it was undertaken by Allom Lovell and Associates and Judy Birmingham (Scott-Virtue 1984a, 1984b) and included monitoring of works within the extant building and excavation of the yard (more details on the excavation are provided in Chapter 2). No catalogue was created due to lack of funding and the assemblage has languished in storage at Museum Victoria ever since. The excavated cesspit is of particular interest here as it was filled with artefacts associated with the Smiths' occupation of the site including tableware, teaware, food storage containers and personal items. The assemblage provides a rare opportunity for the archaeological study of a middle-class domestic site in an urban setting and of cultural capital in this era.

ARCHAEOLOGY OF THE MIDDLE CLASS

Over the past almost 20 years numerous calls have been made for studies on middle-class material culture in Australian historical archaeology (Lawrence 1998:13; Murray and Mayne 2001:103; Karskens and Lawrence 2003:100–101; Crook et al. 2005:27; Crook 2011:592; Murray 2011). It is essential to study the full range of class positions and consumer behaviour in order to characterise assemblages and study class differences (Praetzellis et al. 1988; Karskens and Lawrence 2003:101; Hayes 2014:1). Middle-class sites are subject to archaeological investigation far less frequently than working-class sites as they are most often located in suburban areas where commercial development is less frequent and is less likely to require excavation

for cultural heritage management purposes. However, four notable studies have made important inroads in this area: my work on Viewbank Homestead on Melbourne's outskirts (Hayes 2007, 2008, 2011b, 2014), Quirk's study of Paradise in the Queensland Goldfields (2008a, 2008b), and research at La Trobe University by Lawrence and others on Willoughby Bean's parsonage in regional Victoria (Lawrence et al. 2009) and the aspirational Thomas household at Port Albert (Prossor et al. 2012). These studies partly grew out of the need to contextualise and understand the numerous urban working class assemblages excavated as a result of cultural heritage management compliance (McCarthy 1989; Lydon 1998; Mayne and Lawrence 1998; G. M. H. Consultants 1999; Karskens 1999; Lydon 1999; Karskens 2001; Murray and Mayne 2001; Crook et al. 2003; Crook and Murray 2004; Lampard 2004; Murray 2006; Lampard 2009; Lampard and Staniforth 2011; Murray 2011). Collectively the studies have made important inroads into characterising middle-class assemblages and have provided insights into the role of material culture in social status and social mobility.

In order to expand on this existing research, the *Suburban Archaeology: Approaching an Archaeology of the Middle Class in 19th-Century Melbourne* (DP1093001) Australian Research Council project was initiated. This multidisciplinary project, conducted jointly by La Trobe University, Deakin University and University of Melbourne, sought to understand the construction of middle-class identities in the context of the growth of modern cities by using history, historical archaeology and museum studies to examine material culture. My research for the *Suburban Archaeology* project has re-examined and expanded on my previous work on Viewbank homestead, published earlier in this monograph series (Hayes 2014). In the current volume, which forms part of the same project, I am seeking to extend the study further and begin to look at the multiplicity of Melbourne's middle class – or the internal variety and changing structure of the middle class. As a side note, I realise that Queen Street is urban not suburban but, in the earliest years of the colony when population numbers were smaller than today, areas of the inner city were residential in nature and similar to the suburban areas that evolved later.

Historical archaeologists have predominantly viewed class as a hierarchical scale through which people and their lifestyles can be described based on empirical evidence (Wurst and Fitts 1999:1; Wurst 2006:191, 197; Lawrence and Davies 2011:252–253). In this vein, the four studies on Australian middle-class sites mentioned above have primarily focused on what class can contribute to our understanding of the site itself and how the people living at the site situated themselves within society. As comparisons emerge between these sites and others, the more apparent the internal diversity of the middle class is both in terms of the nature of the sites and the characteristics of the assemblages. As more information is gained a problem emerges: what I might describe as a middle-class site might not fit that description for others. This is largely the result of the constantly changing nature of Australia's middle class in the 19th century. As I see it, this does not need to hinder the study of class nor does it render the concept of class irrelevant in the Australian context. Instead, it creates the opportunity to utilise these differences in examining the noted diversity.

I use the terminology of working, middle and upper class here, but treat these groups as flexible and fluid. My approach to class is not to determine definite class position, nor to create a more accurate description of class in Australia but rather to group like people in order to use the concept of class to examine how individuals were improving their position and the role this played in formulating and changing society. To me it is not so much a hierarchical spectrum but about different modes of life. This approach has its genesis in the works of Giddens (1973) and Bourdieu (1977) which focus on describing different lifestyles and how they relate to social formation, status negotiation and social change. These will be discussed in more detail below.

THE MULTIPLICITY OF MELBOURNE'S MIDDLE CLASS

Melbourne in the 19th century was growing into a vibrant, global city and new arrivals, from elsewhere in Australia and from around the world, were seeking to secure a livelihood and improve their position. The middle class in Melbourne became increasingly diverse with opportunities for social mobility changing considerably over time (Swain 2005:669). The golden period of opportunity for upward mobility was from settlement until the 1880s (Cannon 1975:207–208). Mobility created competition within the middle class, and as the 19th century progressed the Australian middle class became a highly stratified social group with various conflicting interests (Young 2003:10, 14).

This process of redefining the middle class is not a new subject in Australian history. Much has been written about the blurring of class distinctions (Davison 2000:9–10), egalitarianism (Hirst 1988; Thompson 1994:5), and the emergence of a highly stratified middle class (Young 2003). The process of redefining the middle class was hugely influential to Australian society. As previous research has shown, historical archaeology has unique contributions to make in understanding the transformation of the middle class. The role of material culture in transforming society can be explored by accessing the ordinary homes and possessions of the different people who belonged to the middle class in the 19th century.

It is apparent that Melbourne's middle class was made up of a number of distinct groups of people in the 19th century. When examining the internal variety of Melbourne's middle class, I find it useful to group immigrants based on similarities in their class backgrounds, generation, time of arrival in the colony and lifestyle once in the colony. I used this approach with reference to the Martin family in my earlier work on Viewbank homestead and it was useful in terms of not only characterising their material culture but also understanding their position in society (Hayes 2014:3–4). With this approach I am not attempting to create an alternative hierarchy, but rather to group like immigrants in order to examine the formation of the middle class in the new colony.

The Martins were part of a group I termed the 'established middle class' and had a firm position of authority in the colony (Hayes 2014:4). This group was made up of early settlers and colonists of middle class backgrounds who brought their gentility and privilege with them to the new colony. They exploited the pastoral opportunities available in Victoria and became wealthy and influential members of society.

In this monograph I focus on another group, which I term 'aspirational early immigrants'. This distinctly different group was also arriving in Melbourne from the earliest years and predominantly comprised the children and grandchildren of convicts or working-class families from New South Wales and Tasmania who were seeking to improve their position and ultimately achieved their middle-class status over the course of their lives. Many of these arrivals became successful hoteliers, businessmen, merchants, shopkeepers and craftsmen. These 'aspirational early immigrants' were, in spite of their working class or convict backgrounds, seeking entry to the ranks of the middle class (see Russell 1994b:15, 2010:113; Young 2010:136). For the purpose of this study, the material recovered from the Queen Street cesspit provides a representative sample of the material culture of 'aspirational early immigrants' in Melbourne.

The 'established middle class' could claim authority over the title of middle class and sought to establish themselves as a kind of landholding, pastoral aristocracy (Swain 2005:669). However, 'aspirational early immigrants' challenged the 'established middle class' and by doing so began the process of formulating a diverse middle class. Further negotiation of what it meant to belong to the middle class occurred later with the influx of a third major group: those seeking their fortune from the gold rush in the 1850s (Russell 1994b:15, 2010:113; Young 2010:136). The archaeological study of the impact of this third group remains for future study.

The timing of arrivals and characteristics of these groups will be discussed in more detail in the next chapter. By examining these groups and their material culture, similarities and differences can be interrogated in order to understand the multiplicity of Melbourne's middle class and the role of material culture in the formulation of new class structures.

Consumerism and Cultural Capital

The diversity of goods available in Melbourne in the 19th century allowed for decision making. The essential principles in the anthropological study of consumerism are relevant here, as for my previous work on Viewbank (Hayes 2008, 2014:2), namely that goods can be regarded as texts that are open to multiple readings, and that consumer choices have symbolic meaning (Douglas and Isherwood 1978; McKendrick et al. 1982; Appadurai 1986; Miller 1987; Spencer-Wood 1987; McCracken 1988; Friedman 1994; Miller 2008, 2010). Studies of consumerism have been popular in historical archaeology and have further developed ways of viewing the social meanings of commodities in society (e.g. Orser Jr. 1994; Gibb 1996; Wurst and McGuire 1999; Majewski and Schiffer 2001). Consumer studies focus largely on interpreting the intentions, beliefs and behaviours of people in the past.

While Marxist examinations of class focus on what people produce for society (i.e. labourer, clerk, banker etc.), agency theory instead focuses on what people consume. Bourdieu's (1977, 1984) theory of social practice has understandable appeal and applicability in historical archaeology and

has been applied in a number of studies (e.g. Wall 1992; Lawrence 1998:8; Mayne and Lawrence 1998; Shackel 2000:233; Praetzellis and Praetzellis 2001; Russell 2003; Young 2004; Hayes 2008; Rotman 2009; Hayes 2014; Lawrence and Davies 2015). Bourdieu argues that the main determining factor in class is cultural capital, but that social (relationships), economic (wealth) and symbolic (legitimised) capital come into play (see Skeggs 1997:8). Cultural capital is learned predominantly from family, and includes values and tastes which are culturally authorised (Webb et al. 2002:x). Bourdieu (1984:77) emphasises food, furniture and clothing, or what we consume as part of everyday life, as the most important indicator of class distinction. *Habitus* is the term used by Bourdieu (1977) to describe the deliberate and subconscious understanding of the behaviours and practices appropriate to one's place in society. Cultural capital is not imposed, but is continually changing depending on the values and opinions of self and others. Further, goods actively pass on and structure culture.

In relation to class, historical archaeologists have used agency theory predominantly to look at how people in the past sustained, projected and maintained their position in society and what this reveals about social hierarchies and social mobility (see Casella and Croucher 2010:2). It is also possible to go further and look at how consumer choices in turn influence class structure and society.

Bourdieu's (1977, 1984) emphasis is on the reproduction of social hierarchies in current society and the effects of society on individuals. Giddens (1984) goes further with his structuration theory and sees both the structure and agent as influencing social systems. The feedback loop implicit in this enables the study of change and acknowledges that individuals can influence social structures. I draw on both theories in this study in order to examine how the Smiths were defining their position and how this in turn influenced Melbourne society.

As with my study on Viewbank homestead gentility will be linked to cultural capital, and the role of respectability is added to the mix. A number of other researchers in archaeology, history and sociology have usefully linked gentility and respectability with Bourdieu's concept of cultural capital (e.g. Skeggs 1997; Praetzellis and Praetzellis 2001:647; Russell 2003:168; Young 2004). Many of the material goods that play a role as cultural capital are found in the archaeological record and can be interrogated to interpret the values and position of the people who owned them. In turn, material culture can be used to interpret the role of gentility and respectability as cultural capital (see Ames 1978; Goodwin 1999). The interrelationship of these two brands of cultural capital and their potential for understanding class and society will be further developed elsewhere (Sato and Hayes in prep), but the roles of both gentility and respectability are important to understanding cultural capital at Queen Street and will be discussed further below.

GENTILITY AND RESPECTABILITY

Studies of class in Australian historical archaeology have frequently involved discussions of respectability and gentility. The majority focus on the working class and view respectability as a unique and defining characteristic of that group (e.g. Lydon 1993a; Karskens 1999; Lawrence 2000; Lampard 2004). Other studies have looked at gentility as a social strategy in projecting (Quirk 2008b; Lawrence et al. 2009) and/or defending (Hayes 2008, 2014) middle-class status. However, respectability has also been viewed as a social strategy (Lampard and Staniforth 2011) and the terms are sometimes used interchangeably. Collectively, this research shows the diverse approaches to gentility and respectability both by people in the past and by the researcher, and highlights the potential of further developing these concepts for the Australian context where class hierarchies were fluid.

The approach of the researcher to class, gentility and respectability needs to be considered and can be summarised as the emic versus etic issue. From an emic perspective, researchers view these concepts as concrete ideas that existed in the past and that people followed. In this case, research aims to understand how people in the past recognised their class and to reconstruct their motivations and engagement with gentility and respectability as fixed notions. From an etic perspective, the terms are used to describe a cultural phenomenon in the past where our analytical perspective and measurement of engagement with these terms (e.g. income, social position, tastes etc.) are explicitly imposed onto past people in order to address research questions. I take the latter approach. For me the question is not whether class aspirations and adherence to gentility and respectability were intentional, rather, it is about how these concepts can be used in research to examine society.

My approach here is a continuation of the one I developed for research on Viewbank homestead (Hayes 2008, 2014:3–4), where class is used as a concept to explore the similarities and differences between groups of people in order to examine social formation. Bourdieu's (1977, 1984) concept of cultural capital, and in turn gentility and respectability, are used as etic values useful for identifying the roles particular groups played in class formation. This approach acknowledges the effect of the researcher on interpretations and the limitations of descriptions of the past which are subject to the complexities of truth, bias and meaning. It can, of course, be difficult to isolate the role of class in identity and individual consumer choice from other factors such as gender, ethnicity and socio-economic status (Wurst and McGuire 1999; Rotman 2009:1; Casella and Croucher 2010:2–3; Shackel 2010:58–60). However, by taking

an explicitly etic stance it is possible to see that we do not do something because of our class but what we do can be understood using class as a concept.

With the above in mind, I find it useful to conceptualise gentility and respectability as operating separately to class, as particular brands of cultural capital that could be adopted, appropriated or adapted by different groups in different ways for different purposes. Classes are defined quite often by respectability or gentility, but the relational aspects of these are overlooked. How they were intertwined and related to each other is particularly important for debates about the middle class. Here, and in ongoing research (Sato and Hayes in prep; Hayes 2017:6–7), the terms are defined diacritically: that is, each in relation to the other. Respectability in Melbourne society is defined as being determined primarily through possessions and deeds, both of which were not predetermined by familial status or upbringing, and as being strategic in nature with a strong emphasis on materialism. This is in contrast to gentility, which is defined as being defensive in nature with an emphasis on protecting status, and determined by upbringing and manner which cannot be copied or appropriated. There is much overlap in the Victorian era between values and behaviours that constitute gentility and those of respectability: refinement, good taste, manners, morality, religious observance, avoidance of idleness, constructive leisure and domesticity (Russell 1994b:60; Marsden 1998:2; Mitchell 2009:261–266). However, it is the *nature* of each brand of cultural capital that is important here. These definitions have been developed specifically to examine class structure and negotiation in 19th-century Melbourne (see Hayes 2014:2–4, 2017:6–7).

My previous work on Viewbank homestead (Hayes 2008, 2014) found that for the 'established middle class', and families like the Martins, gentility appeared to be inherent and served a distancing function to protect their group from those of non-middle-class backgrounds who were seeking entry to their ranks. In so doing, they also created a sense of inclusion and perpetuated the class system that benefitted them. It is anticipated that the Smiths engaged with gentility and respectability in the 19th century in a way particular to their purpose, and that this will be reflected in their material culture.

METHODS

The interpretations in this study will be based on the reconstruction of the Smiths' household using all available evidence, not just artefacts. The archaeological record is only ever a partial representation of the material culture of people in the past. Variations in deposition patterns, occupation periods, reasons for discard and decomposition of certain materials mean that an assemblage is only ever a sample of a sample.

Personal histories, the home itself and the artefacts will be used together to reconstruct the household to create the most complete possible picture which will then form the basis of interpretation (see Murray 2006).

After presenting the early history of Melbourne, the site and the excavation (Chapter 2), personal histories of the residents both before their arrival in Victoria and once in the colony are used to establish the background, aspirations and success of the residents (Chapter 3). Next, the house and grounds are considered as material culture that can further inform an understanding of life at the house. This will involve a detailed analysis of the spatial layout of the house, the use of rooms and the architecture (Chapter 4). The material culture the Smiths left in their cesspit will then be analysed focusing on life in and about the house: eating and drinking, personal appearance, health and hygiene, recreation and work (Chapter 5). This information will then be integrated (Chapter 6) in an exploration of the daily life and lifestyles of the Smith family. These three branches of evidence and the reconstruction of the household will then form the basis of interpretation of the role cultural capital, and more specifically gentility and respectability, played in the Smiths' rapid rise and how this relates to Melbourne's changing middle class (Chapter 7).

This study provides important comparative material for the archaeological examination of Australia's middle class. The 300 Queen Street site is a rare example of a middle-class urban site accessible for archaeological investigation and provides a unique addition to the studies mentioned above. The Smith family at Queen Street came from very different backgrounds to the Martins at Viewbank, and their material culture provides an excellent opportunity to examine the distinctive way in which these Melbourne immigrants, who I describe as the 'aspirational middle class', were negotiating their position, and to further contribute to understanding the formation of the middle class in Melbourne. As we will see, cultural capital not only aided in propelling John Thomas Smith to his position as Mayor but also, ultimately, pushed boundaries and reinvented the acceptable in Melbourne society.

2
Early Melbourne and 300 Queen Street

The foundational years of Melbourne from the beginning of European settlement until the 1860s form the backdrop of this study. From 1835 the basic village that marked the commencement of settlement grew gradually, until the gold rush in 1851 triggered rapid development towards the global city it would ultimately become (Davison 1978:6). This chapter presents the early Melbourne history pertinent to the Smith family's time at 300 Queen Street, along with details of 300 Queen Street itself and the archaeological investigations at the site.

EARLY MELBOURNE

After three decades of occasional visits and failed settlements, the first permanent European settlement commenced in 1835 (Boyce 2011:9–12). An unsanctioned treaty was made by John Batman and elders of the Wurundjeri to exchange yearly provision of supplies of blankets, knives, tomahawks, mirrors, axes, clothes etc. for approximately 600,000 acres of land (Broome 1984:20; Kociumbas 1992:190–191; Attwood 2009). By this time, the Aboriginal population had already suffered from the effects of introduced diseases, particularly smallpox from Asia, and the British colonists brought tuberculosis, measles and venereal diseases causing countless deaths (Campbell 2002:xii, 216; Shaw 1996:20). Yet disease was not the only risk to the Aboriginal people in Port Phillip. Encounters between settlers and Aboriginal people were often confused and violent (Broome 2005:14). Pastoral settlers displaced Aboriginal people from their land, particularly on Melbourne's fringe, and in many cases Aboriginal people were forced to seek European food in Melbourne (Broome 2005:20–21).

Following the treaty, the grab for land in the Port Phillip district commenced in earnest, conducted initially by squatters from Van Diemens Land (now Tasmania). Shortly after 'overlanders' from New South Wales began to arrive in increasing numbers, following in the footsteps of Major Thomas Mitchell who first made the long and hazardous journey in 1836 (Broome 1984:20). With them travelled ex-convicts who filled the early need for labour.

John Smith arrived in Melbourne in 1837 and was typical of the 'aspirational early immigrants'. This group was made up largely of young people seeking to better themselves, make their fortune and move into the middle class in spite of their convict or working-class backgrounds (Russell

1994b:15, 2010:113; Young 2010:136). For many of them the quest to better their position involved being entrepreneurial in business in order to obtain the wealth required. Many of these arrivals became successful hoteliers, businessmen, merchants, shopkeepers and craftsmen.

While 'overstraiters' and 'overlanders' continued to make the journey, when news of the adventure and fortune that could be had in Port Phillip reached Britain, another wave of immigrants made their way to the colony (Broome 1984:22; Dingle 1984:21–22). A middle-class man who left England for the new colony of Port Phillip could become wealthier and more influential in society (Hayes 2014:7). These early settlers were mostly men of considerable capital, and arrived with their families and servants. They went first to Sydney and then within a short period of arriving made the trip to Port Phillip (Broome 1984:20–21). In addition to these middle-class immigrants, and in response to severe labour shortages by the mid-1840s, the British working class, and in particular the agricultural poor, were actively encouraged to migrate (Broome 1984:40–41; Boyce 2011:155–156).

During the first years of the Port Phillip district conditions were hard. Melbourne was a 'primitive village' (Davison 1978:6) and services were limited (**Figure 6**). By 1840, however, Melbourne had a population of around 4,000 and had become an administrative centre servicing the pastoral interests of the Port Phillip district (Brown-May 1998:1–2). In spite of an economic depression in the early 1840s, by 1843 shops and hotels were steadily emerging (Dingle 1984:27; Priestley 1984:23–24). From the outset, the settlement lauded respectability and distanced itself from the 'convict stain' in spite of the undeniable presence of convicts and ex-convicts in the district (Boyce 2011:56).

In 1851, the Port Phillip district became the separate Colony of Victoria, now a state of Australia. The first discoveries of gold were made soon after, bringing great upheaval and transformation to the colony (Cannon 1971:180). The gold also brought a fresh influx of arrivals with working-class backgrounds who were seeking their fortune and the opportunity to establish themselves in the new society (Hayes 2014:20). The population increased from 29,000 in 1850 to 125,000 ten years later (Davison 1978:6). The gold rushes continued throughout the 19th century, but were declining in influence from the 1870s (Serle 1971:1). From this

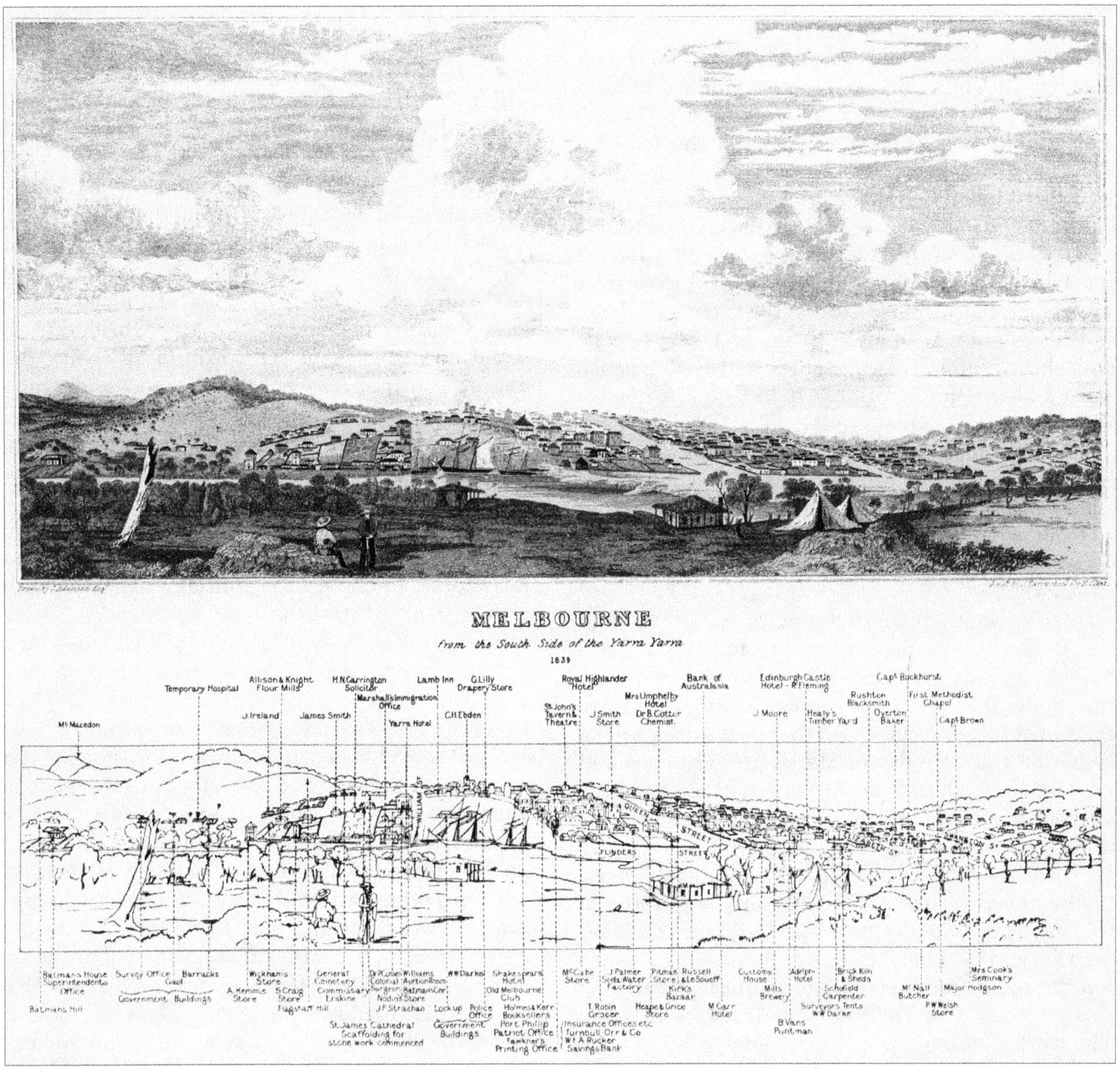

Figure 6: Melbourne from the south side of the Yarra Yarra, 1839. Also showing 'J Smith Store' (Creator: J. Carmichael; Engraver: J. Adamson 1841; Source: State Library of Victoria, www.slv.vic.gov.au).

time, wool, wheat, and manufacturing were the primary industries in Victoria (Serle 1971:45–85). Two periods of depression affected the colony in the first three decades: one in the early 1840s and another in the 1850s (Broome 1984:35, 87). In spite of this, the legacy of the gold rushes was that they enabled Melbourne to grow into a commercial centre, not only because of the wealth the gold created, but from the demand for services required by a growing population (Davison 1978:11). By 1891, Melbourne's population had expanded to 491,000 and it had become a true metropolis: a bustling, viable, global city (Serle 1971:77; Davison 1978:7).

Robert Hoddle established his grid of streets for Melbourne in early 1837 and initial land sales took place in the centre of Melbourne in June (Priestley 1984:19–20). By 1839 these allotments were again subdivided and sold at huge profits (Annear 1995:31–33). Along the northern boundary of Melbourne was

a wooded hill, and in 1840 a flagstaff was erected on its summit (Priestley 1984:20). The western end of Bourke, Lonsdale and La Trobe Streets was fashionably residential up until the late 1850s when the expansion of the town pushed professional and business people to move to the suburbs. In 1849, in this fashionable area, John Thomas Smith built his residence at 300 Queen Street, situated one block to the east of the flagstaff. The earlier houses in this area were surrounded by gardens and orchards, sometimes with a paddock; however, the Smith's residence was one of the first true town houses fronting directly onto the street. His neighbours included landowner Sir William Clarke and famous surgeon T.N. Fitzgerald (Priestley 1984:26–27). Later, this area of Melbourne became the centre for government buildings (Nigel Lewis and Associates 1982:20–21).

300 QUEEN STREET

John Thomas Smith purchased the lot at 300 Queen Street in 1847 after its initial subdivision. To build his residence Smith employed architect Charles Laing, who he had earlier engaged to build the Queen's Theatre (*The Argus*, 17 January 1931:7). Laing issued a tender notice for bricklayers, carpenters, painters and plasterers to build a dwelling for Smith (*Port Phillip Herald*, 22 February 1848). In 1850 the first rate book entry lists four rooms finished and four rooms unfinished. By 1851, the rate book records a house with eight rooms and four cellars, and shortly after this a stables and coach house were added (PROV, VPRS 5702/P0, MCC Bourke Ward Rate Books, 1847–1851).

The dwelling was a two storey brick stuccoed house on a bluestone base. The 1855 Bibbs Map shows two outbuildings: a long stable building and a small square building on the south-east corner (Nigel Lewis and Associates 1982:23; Scott-Virtue 1984a:4).

In 1852 Smith submitted a notice of intention to the Public Works Department 'to finish the office building to my dwelling house situate in Queen Street and that I am to be my own Master builder of the works to be executed and that said works will be begun on the 14th day of March' (Nigel Lewis and Associates 1982:9). It is unclear whether this was an additional free standing building or alterations to the existing dwelling.

In 1858 Smith wished to add additional space to 300 Queen Street apparently for the purpose of converting it into a commercial building. A tender for a 'large addition to the residence of John Thomas Smith' under the direction of architect David Ross was advertised in *The Argus* on 15 January 1858. The work was undertaken by builder John Morton and involved the removal of the roof in order to add a second storey (Nigel Lewis and Associates 1982:10). After the extension, the rate books indicate that the house had 12 rooms (PROV, VPRS 5702/P0, MCC Bourke Ward Rate Books, Unit 10, 1859). Sometime between September and November 1859 the Smiths moved out of the residence and leased it to the government for use as the Treasury building (Nigel Lewis and Associates 1982:10). This building is one of only a few from pre-1850s Melbourne that remains extant, and is the largest dwelling surviving in the CBD from the pastoral era.

From 1860 to 1875, Smith leased the building to the government for the use of various departments including the Treasury, Board of Agriculture, Department of Mines, Central Board for the Protection of Aborigines, and Geological Survey (PROV, VPRS 5708/P9, MCC Rate Books, 1861–1871; Nigel Lewis and Associates 1982:11). Smith was the Minister of Mines from 1869 to 1870, so he may have had an office in his former house at this time (Nigel Lewis and Associates 1982:12). In a change of pace, from 1871 to 1880, the building was occupied by Robert Stewart, confectioner/jam and peel manufacturer (PROV, VPRS 5708/P9, MCC Rate Books, 1871–1875).

After Smith's death in 1879, the property passed to the J.T. Smith Trust. Stewart maintained occupancy along with T. Phillips, who conducted a boarding house in three flats, and David Munro, who operated a machine yard on the land. Then, in 1881, David Munro purchased the house and property. From 1875 until 1882 David Munro was listed as the ratepayer on the lot south of 300 Queen Street, which included a machine yard, offices, a shed and workshop. With Munro as owner the building continued as a boarding house, clothing manufacturers and Munro's offices (PROV, VPRS 5708/P9, MCC Rate Books, 1879–1888). Munro added a three storey warehouse and factory to the rear of the site in 1882.

David Munro, born in Scotland in 1844, was an engineer, speculator and contractor. He arrived in Victoria in 1854 and initially worked with his father as a blacksmith and contractor. After becoming insolvent in 1869, Munro started his own engineering and machinery business. He married Sarah Elizabeth Sydenham in 1871 and they had three sons and two daughters. During the railway boom of the 1870s and 1880s, Munro was one of the largest employers in the colony. He built the Queens Bridge and Princes Bridge, in addition to a number of railways. He also sold sawmilling, threshing and mining equipment and owned extensive property. Like many others affected by the land-boom collapse, Munro's success took a dramatic downturn from the late 1880s. Shares in Munro's company fell to almost nothing, along with the market price of his land. He was declared bankrupt in 1890. The family moved to a small cottage in Parkville where Munro died in 1898, aged 54 (Cannon 1966:228, 1974:311–312).

Munro's wife Sarah Elizabeth became the registered proprietor of the property in August 1888. The property was subsequently vacant from 1890 to 1896 when the Land Mortgage Bank assumed ownership after foreclosure on the mortgage. From then on the property was used as a boarding house and various other businesses until it was purchased by the Victorian State Government in 1950. At this time all of the buildings on the site except for the Smith's residence were demolished. The building was occupied by the Mental Hygiene Authority from 1954 to 1976 and was then vacant until 1982 when preparations commenced for renovations as corporate offices (Nigel Lewis and Associates 1982:4; Scott-Virtue 1984b:6).

ARCHAEOLOGICAL INVESTIGATIONS AT 300 QUEEN STREET

The archaeological investigation of the site in 1983 was conducted by Allom Lovell and Associates and Judy Birmingham with Lee Scott-Virtue as

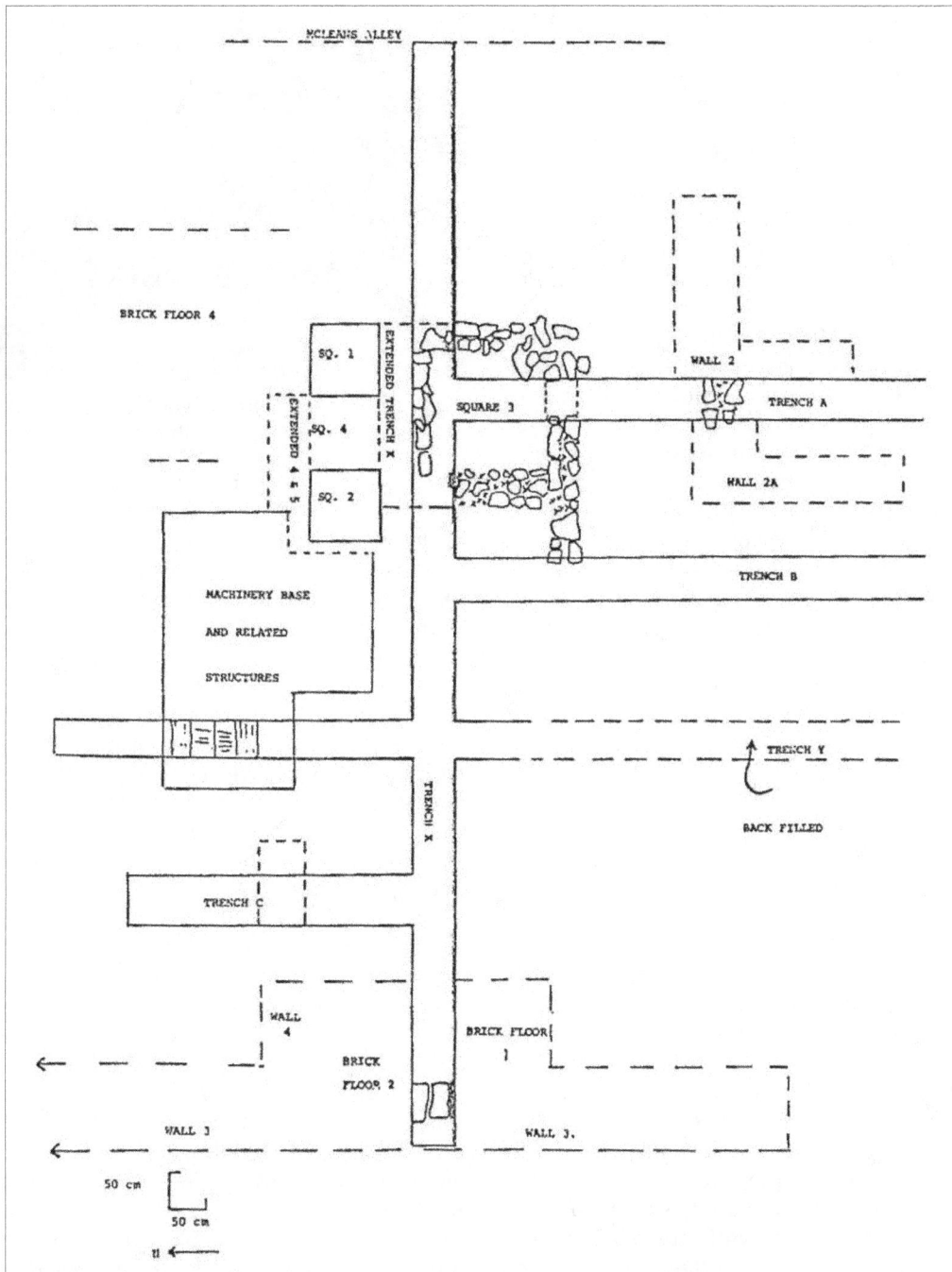

Figure 7: Excavation plan showing backhoe trenches and location of cesspit (Square 3) (Source: Scott-Virtue 1984b:30).

the primary sub-consultant. The investigation focused on the extant building and grounds, and was overseen by the Department of Housing and Construction. The project aimed to protect and conserve the heritage value of the building during renovations and the construction of additional offices on the land behind the building. The work sought to preserve items *in situ* where possible and only to remove items where this was necessary for preservation (Scott-Virtue 1984a:1–2). Excavations took place over a two-month period, while the investigation of the building itself was conducted in conjunction with renovation work over 12 months.

The excavations in the rear yard included two preliminary test trenches excavated by backhoe which revealed that prior building works had significantly disturbed the 19th-century cultural material. Three additional backhoe trenches were then excavated to identify areas of greatest potential (**Figure 7**). This work identified the remains of a 'cistern' and footings and further controlled excavation was carried out to investigate these features. After the completion of these excavations, monitoring continued during the construction work and recovered some fragmentary artefacts (Scott-Virtue 1984a:7).

The archaeological work on the Smiths' residence drew on an earlier report on the architectural and cultural significance of the site, which had detailed and mapped the rooms within the residence (Nigel Lewis and Associates 1982:65–89). The first stage of the investigation of the building itself involved an assessment of the conservation requirements of the building. The second phase involved weekly site visits, along with additional site visits when requested by the Department of Housing and Construction. Investigations in the extant building focused on conservation recommendations rather than archaeological objectives. The work uncovered two forms of evidence. First, evidence of the type and sequence of alterations to the building, and second, artefacts found in floor and roof spaces. Artefacts found within the house were not removed unless they were likely to be disturbed by building works. Evidence of a servant bell system in the form of copper wires and brass mountings was also uncovered (Scott-Virtue 1984a:8–9, 18, 21).

The most substantial archaeological evidence from the grounds related to the Smith phase of occupation and included two buildings interpreted by the excavators to be the stables and coach house listed in the early rate books. The stables were probably built in 1853 with a coach house added in 1854. The 1855 map of inner Melbourne created by Thomas Franklin Bibbs (State Library of Victoria, www.slv.vic.gov.au) shows a long, rectangular building behind the residence and a small square building at the back of the block (Scott-Virtue 1984a:19, 1984b:8–10). The excavations did not conclusively reveal the extent or construction of these buildings, but they had bluestone footings, and brick fragments were recovered. Both buildings disappeared from the rate books by 1863 and it is possible that they were removed or repurposed at this time (Scott-Virtue 1984b:8–9).

The excavators identified a roughly square bluestone pit of unclear purpose within what they identified as the stable building (**Figure 7**). The pit had a yellow clay base with overlying timbers and walls which extended beyond the pit itself suggesting it was part of a building. Scott-Virtue (1984a:19) suggested that this was initially used as a water cistern and subsequently to discard rubbish after its original function became obsolete. However, the dimensions of the structure do not support this interpretation, as the water storage capacity would have been minimal. It is argued here that the cistern was in fact a cesspit housed within a purpose-specific building. Cesspits were in use in Melbourne until the late 1870s (Hayes and Minchinton 2016), and Macleans Lane to the rear of the property would have facilitated night soil removal.

The square pit was lined with mortared bluestone and had an internal size of approximately 1.5m x 1.5m with a depth of 1.6m (**Figure 8**) (Scott-Virtue 1984b:30–31) and is consistent with bluestone

Figure 8: Image of the cesspit from the original report (Source: Scott-Virtue 1984b:47).

cesspits at Little Lon (see Godden Mackay Logan et al. 2004; Hayes and Minchinton 2016). Previous research on the history and archaeology of cesspits in early Melbourne suggests that this pit was constructed prior to 1861 (Hayes and Minchinton 2016). At this time, the Central Board of Health released a circular specifying that cesspits must meet a particular set of parameters relating to construction, dimensions and waterproofing with puddled clay. Although the cesspit at Queen Street had a clay base, this is likely to have been the naturally occurring clay underlying the pit rather than waterproofing. There is no mention in the excavation reports of the clay extending to the top of the pit as specified in the circular. The pit is also larger than the bluestone pits recommended in the circular, so that the combined evidence suggests a construction date prior to 1861 for the cesspit.

The excavation of square 3 comprised the interior of the cesspit, which was excavated to its base at a depth of 1.6m. Each stratigraphic layer (**Figure 9**) was excavated as one unit except for heavily concentrated cultural deposits which were removed in arbitrary spits. All soil was sieved through 3mm and 5mm mesh. Two artefact deposits were identified: the 'lower deposit' was near the base of the cesspit while the 'upper deposit' was resting in a depression over the top of the cesspit extending into squares 2, 4 and extended 4 and 5 (**Figure 7**). In 1853 a new stable was constructed over the top of the cesspit. It appears that the pit ceased being used for its intended purpose at this time and the empty hole was subsequently used for rubbish by the Smiths. Directly overlying the lower deposit was a layer of timber off-cuts, scattered bluestone and brick fragments with a second layer of sterile sandy soil over this which appears to have been purposefully added in order to fill the cesspit. This created a clear demarcation between the lower and upper deposits of artefacts. Scott-Virtue notes that there was little resemblance between the two deposits (Scott-Virtue 1984b:31, 46–48, 67), and argues that the lower deposit comprised domestic material relating to the Smith phase of occupation

EAST FACE OF CISTERN

UPPER CULTURAL
DEPOSIT

WALL 1A

LOWER CULTURAL
DEPOSIT

TRENCH X

10cm

10cm

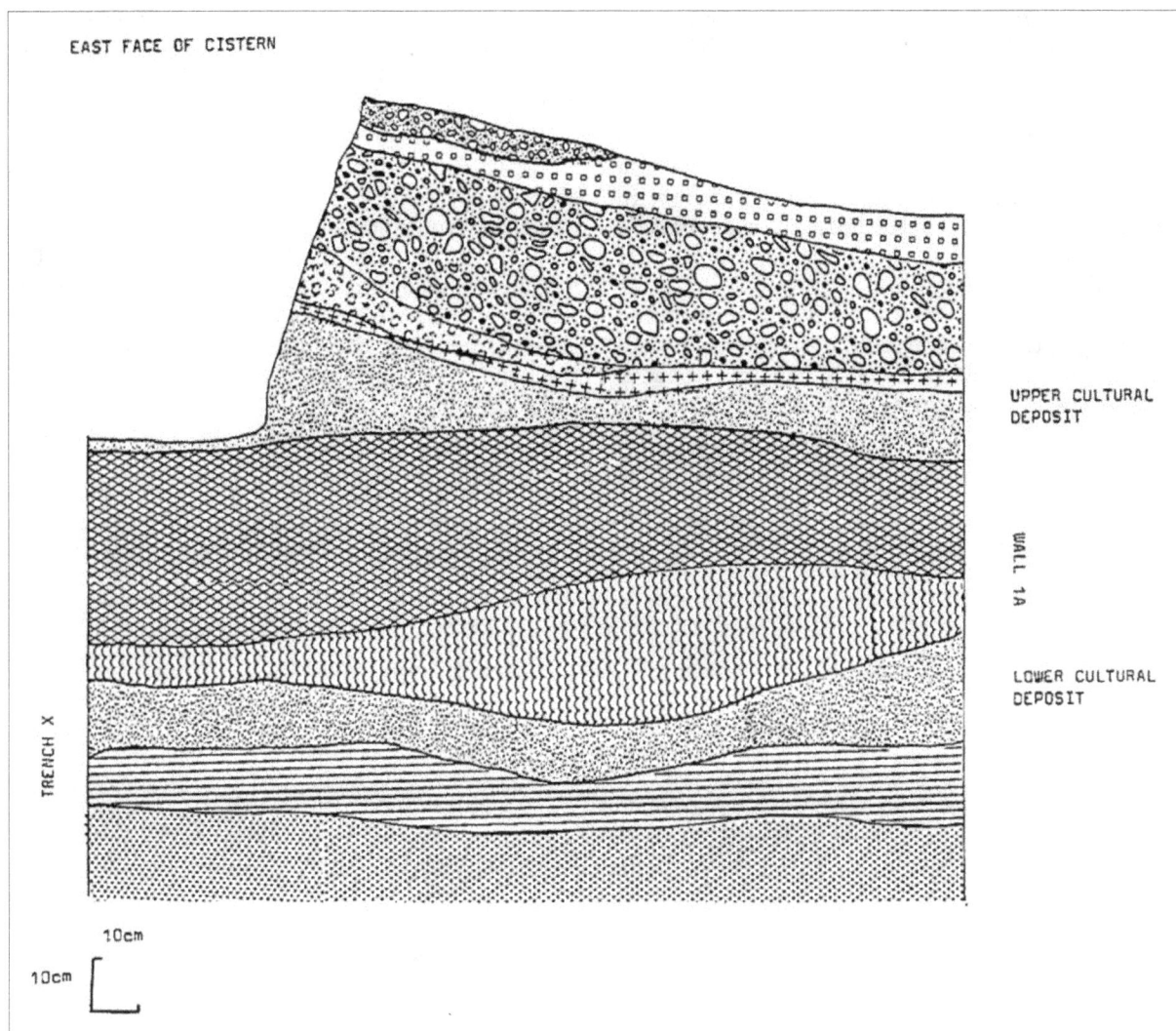

Figure 9: Stratigraphy of the cesspit showing the locations of the upper and lower cultural deposits (Source: Scott-Virtue 1984b:28).

and the upper deposit to the use of the site as offices from 1860 until around 1875.

Excavations did not recover all boundaries of the stables and coach house so it is difficult to determine the full extent or nature of these buildings. Later buildings on the property were also uncovered by the excavation and included a red brick and bluestone building constructed for Munro in 1882–1883 for the manufacture of machinery and a later 1950s building (Scott-Virtue 1984a:19).

Artefacts

The assemblage recovered from the lower deposit within the cesspit is a unique and valuable example of material culture from this early period of Melbourne's history. The assemblage includes domestic ceramics, glass, faunal material, seeds, leather, clay pipes and assorted small finds. No mention of artefact discard or sampling was made in the report, other than for building materials. The intactness of the artefacts would suggest that

all artefact fragments from the lower deposit were retained.

The time limit for the completion of the original report meant that there was very little scope for working on the assemblage. Research was further hindered by the lack of comparative material and literature available in the early 1980s for identifying artefacts (Scott-Virtue 1984b:52). Scott-Virtue (1984a:21) recommended that 'a catalogue be prepared and published by the Commonwealth Government of the archaeological artefacts from the cistern' and that 'the artefacts be deposited in an appropriate public institution and undergo professional conservation, curation and display'.

Time constraints and lack of funding meant that the assemblage was deposited with Museum Victoria in a miscellaneous array of unlabelled cardboard boxes with many or all artefacts unwashed (the report states that the ceramics had a preliminary wash but that further cleaning was required) and without a catalogue (Scott-Virtue 1984b:55). The report provides some information on artefacts recovered from the cesspit including summary tables of artefacts, brief descriptions of some artefact types and a discussion of the assemblage. The majority of artefacts were labelled only with the site name, context information and date. The assemblage was not accessioned into Museum Victoria's collection, so no records existed for it in the Museum's database, KE EMu. No conservation had been undertaken on the assemblage, nor had it been utilised for display.

At some stage, a Masters student commenced research on the assemblage. Many artefacts were washed, sorted, conjoined and re-bagged as part of this research. Unfortunately no project report or catalogue is available from this work. As part of that project a number of artefacts were labelled with object numbers (for example BTL-SS 10, MISC-SS 4). This was the only prior research work conducted on the assemblage.

300 Queen Street holds an important place in Melbourne's early history, being one of the earliest residential town houses built within the city centre, and one of the oldest buildings still standing. The assemblage had languished in boxes in spite of its historical and archaeological value, and needed rigorous analysis, carefully contextualised against the personal histories of the people who discarded the goods.

Personal Histories

The trajectories of the lives of the Smith family will be examined in this chapter using historical sources in order to establish the family as typical of the 'aspirational early immigrants' group. John Thomas Smith's convict roots are discussed, showing how he gradually moved beyond his past to become Mayor of Melbourne, a wealthy business man and property owner. Ellen Smith's Irish antecedents will also be explored, along with the fortunes of the next generation in marriage and occupation. By tracking personal milestones, the aspirations and successes of members of the Smith family are set out as the basis for the discussion later in the monograph. When combined with the material record in this way, such personal histories can be used to explore the changing nature of class in society (Mrozowski 2006:1).

JOHN THOMAS SMITH

John Thomas Smith (**Figure 10**) was a currency lad born in Sydney in 1816 to a convict father and Sydney born Elizabeth Smith, herself the daughter of convicts (BDM NSW V181640161Bb/1816). John Smith was a Scottish shoemaker who was sentenced to transportation for life at the age of 19 for theft (UK, Prison Hulk Registers and Letter Books, 1802–1849, HO9 Piece 4). He arrived in Australia on the *Admiral Gambier* in 1808 and by the time of the Census in 1828 he had received an Absolute Pardon and was living in Pitt Street, Sydney (SANSW, 1828 NSW Census L-T NRS 1272). John Smith married Elizabeth Jennings-Biggs in July 1815 (BDM NSW V181517803Am/1815 & V1815167 7m/1815). She was born in the colony in 1796 to convict parents William Biggs and Mary Jennings, both English (Smee 1981). Elizabeth died aged 58 in Sydney in 1854 (BDM NSW 1447d/1854, vol. 106).

John and Elizabeth Smith had ten children, and John Thomas Smith was the eldest (Smee 1981). He was baptised at St Phillip's Sydney, and educated at W. Cape's School (*The Argus*, 31 January 1879:6). As a teenager, Smith was apprenticed to Beaver & Co., builders and joiners, but when the business failed in 1833 his indentures were cancelled (*Leader*, 14 March 1863:1). Then came the first in a progression of career opportunities that facilitated Smith's move up in society; first of all he became a bank clerk, before taking up a position in the colonial store (*The Argus*, 31 January 1879:6). It was not long before Smith set off for Melbourne, arriving in 1837 on the

James Watt, the first steamer to travel from Sydney to Port Phillip (Hetherington 1964:89). In the Port Phillip District he began as an assistant teacher at the Church of England Aboriginal Mission Station on the Yarra River earning £40 a year, but he did not stay long before taking up a position as clerk and storekeeper to John Hodgson, the future Mayor of Melbourne (Hetherington 1964:89; Eastwood 1976:150; *The Age*, 18 August 1856:3; *Leader*, 14 March 1863:1).

Smith married Ellen Pender in 1839 when he was 23 and she was 19 (BDM VIC 4166m/1839). Ellen was Irish Catholic, and the daughter of a publican – a scandalous combination for a Church of England man with aspirations at this time. While his marriage to Ellen was frowned upon by some, it was a match that ultimately started Smith on the road to wealth via the lucrative occupation of publican (Eastwood 1976:150–151). His father-in-law, Michael Pender, was an innkeeper and it became the family trade with Smith's brother-in-law Robert Brettagh also running hotels. Smith took over the Adelphi Hotel in Flinders Lane from Brettagh in 1841 and St John's Tavern in Queen Street in 1844 (PROV, VPRS 7/P0, Department of the Treasurer Inward Correspondence (Bound), Index to inward correspondence regarding publicans 1838–1855).

Figure 10: John Thomas Smith (Source: Parliament of Victoria Re-Member https://www.parliament.vic.gov.au/re-member/details/730-john-thomas-smith)

Building on these initial successful business enterprises, Smith employed Charles Laing to build the Queen's Theatre Royal next to St John's Tavern in 1845 (*The Argus*, 17 January 1931:7) (**Figure 11**). The theatre was a brick and stone building that could house 1,200 people (Colligan 2005:583). It was Melbourne's first purpose-built theatre and although thefts were often reported as taking place in the pit (e.g. *Port Phillip Gazette and Settler's Journal*, 13 January 1847:2), it was rarely criticised for immorality in the early years other than by John Thomas Smith's political opponents (e.g. *The Argus*, 19 September 1848:2). Smith applied for the third time for a circus to be attached to the Queen's Theatre in 1849 (*The Argus*, 13 April 1849), but approval was never given.

The Queen's Theatre hosted performances of varying quality and seriousness, and its patrons were not always socially respectable, but still Smith attempted to cater for more genteel tastes (*Leader*, 14 March 1863:1; *The Argus*, 18 May 1864:5; *The Australian News for Home Readers*, 25 January 1864:14; *The Age*, 5 February 1855:5). He reserved the dress circle for gentlefolk, prohibited smoking in the theatre and had street lighting installed on Queen Street (Finn 1888:478; Eastwood 1976:150–151). Miss Catherine Hayes hosted and performed in a Grand Concert with music from Mendelssohn and Bellini in 1854 (*The Argus*, 31 October 1854:8) among other performances throughout the year. Corroborees were staged and were well attended

Figure 11: The Queen's Theatre, c.1880–1885 (Creator: Charles Samuel Bennett; Source: State Library of Victoria, www.slv.vic.gov.au).

(*The Argus*, 31 January 1925:8). *The Argus* describes a perhaps more typical evening's entertainment at the theatre in 1855:

On Friday evening the theatre was crowded on the occasion of Mr. Mungall's benefit. The pieces were, the drama of "Gilderoy," the farce of "The Irish Tutor," and a pantomime called "Harlequin Hoax." Mr Mungall's performance of the Herdsman was intelligent and clever, and as a Clown in the pantomime

Figure 12: A Group of City Fathers, 1862 (John Thomas Smith third from right) (Publisher: Alfred Martin Ebsworth; Source: State Library of Victoria, www.slv.vic.gov.au).

he exhibited proofs of the versatility of his talent (*The Argus*, 15 May 1855:5).

The Queen's Theatre was often used as a fund-raising venue for various causes including supporting the wives and orphans of deceased Brothers of the Odd Fellows of the Manchester Unity (*The Argus*, 18 September 1848:2), a Licensed Victualler's Amateur Benefit Performance for the war relief fund (*The Argus*, 6 October 1854:5) and for the benefit of survivors of the *Cataraqui* shipwreck (*The Argus*, 23 April 1927:8).

There were also performances that caused controversy. 'Rolla', a satirical take on Eureka, was critically reported in *The Age* (20 January 1855:6) triggering a government review presaging a possible ban (*The Age*, 23 January 1855:5). The ban was rejected.

Smith's political career began in 1842 when he won the seat for Bourke Ward on the first Melbourne Town Council; he was a councillor for the rest of his life. He became Mayor of Melbourne in 1851 and was re-elected seven times; he was also a member of both houses of Parliament at different times (De Serville 1991:209). Smith was a conservative politician (*Leader*, 14 March 1863:1) and steadfast when it came to upholding law and order. He strongly opposed the reduction of the miners' licence fee in 1853, and as Mayor at the time of the Eureka uprising responded by enlisting all able-bodied men as special constables to protect Melbourne against a perceived threat from marauding miners. Smith was also a magistrate who was considered fair and kind in his judgements (*Bendigo Advertiser*, 31 January 1879:3; *Leader*, 14 March 1863:1; Hetherington 1964:93–94; Eastwood 1976:150–151). He was regarded as one of Melbourne's city fathers (**Figure 12**).

Smith was deeply concerned with public interests. A passage from the *Bendigo Advertiser* sums up his charitable contributions:

> A trustee of St. John's Church and schools, St. Matthew's Church and school lands, Melbourne; St. Thomas's Church and schools, Essendon ... trustee of the Victorian Savings Bank, a member of the Central Board of Health, chairman of the Board of Visitors to the Metropolitan Lunatic Asylums, and the Retreats at Cremorne and Northcote. ... The Benevolent Asylum and Orphan Asylum inmates are mainly indebted to Mr. Smith for the home they enjoy. The Melbourne Hospital, which will bear comparison with any similar institution in the world, has been largely benefited by Mr. Smith and his family (*Bendigo Advertiser*, 31 January 1879:3).

He also backed the eight-hour movement, providing financial support to the cause in the 1850s (*Geelong Advertiser*, 16 September 1859:3; Eastwood 1976:150–151). He was an employer, but still

Figure 13: Funeral of the Late John Thomas Smith, MLA, 1879 (Publisher: David Syme & Co.; Source: State Library of Victoria, www.slv.vic.gov.au).

donated the use of the Queen's Theatre for the Eight Hours meetings throughout 1856 (*The Age*, 27 March 1856:3).

Smith had a keen interest in property. In the centre of Melbourne, along with the Queen's Theatre and 300 Queen Street, Smith owned a number of pubs at various times, small shops, cottages and the Treasury Building in William Street (PROV, VPRS 28/P2, Unit 89, 17 April 1879; Nigel Lewis and Associates 1982:9). He also owned a number of properties in the Melbourne suburbs of Hawthorn, Williamstown, Ascot Vale, North Melbourne, West Melbourne and Carlton (LUV GLL 1st and 2nd Series Indexes). Around Victoria he owned shops, residences, farms and pastoral properties in Sandridge, Mornington, Maribyrnong, Cranbourne and Lyndhurst among others (PROV, VPRS 28/P2, Unit 89, 17 April 1879). He also owned stations on the Darling River in New South Wales and ten runs in the Warrego District, Queensland (PROV, VPRS 28/P2, Unit 89, 11 February 1881).

The family moved from 300 Queen Street to Mount Alexander Road, Flemington in 1859, possibly with a brief stay in South Yarra in between. The area was a genteel farming district in the 1860s and it would appear that the family were approximating a version of the lifestyle of the wealthy landholder. Smith also owned a 'farm' at Frankston, a healthy seaside retreat (*The Argus*, 31 January 1879:6).

Smith died from cancer at age 63 in January 1879. As **Figure 13** shows, Smith's funeral was conducted with a certain grandeur and public ceremony. He was the provincial grand master of the Kent Lodge of Freemasons by the time of his death and had remained an active member of the Church of England. Smith was buried in the Anglican section of the Melbourne General Cemetery (*The Argus*, 31 January 1879:6). His estate was valued for probate at £42,000 (PROV, VPRS 28/P2, Unit 89, 24 April 1879). In his will he left the Ascot Vale property to his eldest son, the Moonee Ponds side of the property to his wife Ellen, remaining money after the sale of his station in New South Wales to his son Sydney, his half share of his Queensland property to sons Harrie and George, and part shares of the Frankston, Queen Street and Elizabeth Street properties to his wife and each of his children (PROV, VPRS 7591/P2, Unit 46).

ELLEN SMITH (NÉE PENDER)

As is frequently the case for women of the 19th century, there is far less historical detail available on the life and accomplishments of Ellen Smith than of her husband. Ellen was the daughter of Michael Pender and Elizabeth Dalton. Pender was born in 1789 in Wicklow, Ireland and Elizabeth in Kildare, Ireland in 1792. Ellen's parents married in Wicklow in 1815 aged 26 and 23 respectively. The Pender family arrived in Hobart Town as free settlers from Dublin in 1833 (AOT *Reports of ships arrivals with lists of passengers*; Film Number: *SLTX/AO/MB/1*; Series Number: *MB2/39/1/1*), although Michael Pender's death certificate places him there in 1828 (BDM VIC 2026d/1873). The Pender's four children were born prior to their migration to Australia and the family stayed together in Tasmania (BDM VIC 7986d/1886, 2026d/1873). The Penders' son, William, went to Port Phillip in 1835, with the rest of the family following in 1839 (*The Argus*, 4 January 1868:5–6).

The Penders were among Melbourne's first publicans with Elizabeth running their hotel, the Shamrock in Little Flinders Street. Pender worked constructing roads with his bullock team and via these enterprises they quickly amassed significant wealth. Convinced by the riches to be made in a drinking house, Pender encouraged his sons-in-law to also become publicans (Hetherington 1964:92).

After Elizabeth's death in 1857 at age 65, Pender married again two more times; first to Mary Ryan and then to Mary Finn. Pender was considered a gentleman and his death notice states that he was 'an old and much respected colonist, dating from the foundation of the colony ...' (*The Argus*, 29 March 1873:2).

Ellen was the eldest of the Penders' four children. Born in 1820 in Kildare, Ireland, she migrated to Australia with her family at around age 13. She was 19 when they made the move to Port Phillip and she married Smith the same year (BDM NSW 537 Vol 23B/1839). Like her husband, Ellen had benevolent interests, including the Lying-In Hospital (*The Argus*, 15 December 1856:5, 7 July 1860:1). After Smith's death, Ellen remained at Flemington and died there aged 66 (BDM VIC 7986d/1886).

CHILDREN

John Thomas and Ellen Smith's 11 children were born between 1840 and 1861 in Melbourne. John Thomas Thorold was the eldest, born the year after the Smith's marriage (BDM VIC 12332b/1840). He was followed by Helen Elizabeth, James, William Charles, Sydney, Henry William and Jane (BDM VIC 16707b/1842, 13495b/1843, 14258b/1845, 14944b/1846, 16427b/1848 and 17209b/1850). Charles Melbourne, Catherine and Louise were born while they were living at 300 Queen Street (BDM VIC 19099b/1853, 19100b/1855 and 7520d/1930). George was the youngest, born in 1859 after the family moved to Flemington (*The Age*, 5 December 1859:4; BDM QLD B35080d/1921). In common with the era, the couple lost two young children: a stillborn in 1858 and William Charles died aged 5 months (*The Age*, 13 July 1858:4; BDM VIC 4081d/1845).

With few options for making an independent living, marriage was the single most important event of the Smith girls' lives. Helen, Catherine, Louise and Jane (Fanny) all married. Helen, the eldest daughter, married Charles Hope Nicolson, the Scottish born Superintendent of Police, who lived in Collins Street in 1861. Nicolson was 31, but Helen was just 19 and permission had to be given by her parents for her to marry (BDM VIC 1309m/1861). Catherine had just turned 20 when she married and also required permission, which was granted by her father. She married Thomas Prout Webb, a Barrister at Law residing in Kew, in July 1875 and had three children (BDM VIC 2609m/1875, 3390d/1943). Louise and Stanhope Edward Dunne O'Connor were wed at Benalla in November 1879. While her wedding certificate states that she was 21, her death certificate records her age at marriage as 18. It is possible that she lied about her age, a common practice at the time, to avoid the need for parental permission. O'Connor was an officer of police at Benalla and socially not quite the match of her sisters' suitors (BDM VIC 3790m/1879). The couple had five children (BDM VIC 7520d/1930). Fanny married George Walter Staples, a stock and share broker, in 1875, and had two children in Ballarat before the family went to live in England (BDM VIC 2608m/1875, 6533b/1877, 6912b/1879; 1911 England Census London, Strand District 13, RG14, Piece 1196).

The story of the Smiths' six sons is a mix of success and tragedy. John Thomas Thorold, the eldest son, was educated in England and went on to become a barrister and Crown Prosecutor (*The Argus*, 10 December 1870:1). He married Ellen Mary Stubbs in 1861 but they had no children (BDM VIC 9638d/1901; De Serville 1991:438). The eldest son was expected to support the unmarried or widowed women of the family in the event of a patriarch's death (Russell 1994a:149). For this reason it was John Thomas Thorold who received the lion's share of the inheritance upon Smith's death including the house on 17 acres at Ascot Vale. John Thomas Thorold was responsible for the upkeep of the family home at Flemington and providing for his mother after his father's death (PROV, VPRS 28/P0, Unit 393). John Thomas Thorold died aged 62 at Shoreham, Flinders and was buried in the Melbourne General Cemetery (BDM VIC 9638d/1901).

Both James and Sydney were employed in operating Smith's Gundabooka Station on the Darling River in New South Wales. James lived there for 10 years before becoming paralysed and returning to the family home in Flemington where he died three years later. He never married (*The*

Argus, 28 May 1878:1; BDM VIC 5228d/1878). Sydney, at the time of his marriage age 27, was listed as a squatter and gentleman. He married Mary Petty in Melbourne in 1876 and they had three children (BDM VIC 541m/1876, 5506b/1878, 19806b/1881, 26539b/1892). Sydney died at his home in St Kilda in 1918 aged 72 (BDM VIC 6759d/1918).

Henry William, known as Harrie, never married and lived with his mother for a number of years until her death. Ellen left her share of the Frankston property and a paddock at Ascot Vale to Harrie because he was 'not as well off as his brothers and sisters and because she had a desire to better [his] position' (PROV, VPRS 28/P0, Unit 393, Affidavit Harrie Smith 16 September 1886). At the time of his death, aged 45, he was the secretary of the Victoria Amateur Turf Club (BDM VIC 10455d/1895). Charles Melbourne also died young, aged 20, from an accident that led to a traumatic femoral aneurysm and septicaemia (BDM VIC 10487d/1874).

The Smiths' youngest son George went on to become a medical practitioner. He lived and studied in England where he married Maud Phyllis Matthews and had two children (1911 England Census Essex, Wivenhoe, District 199, Schedule 268, Piece 10333). Upon returning to Australia, George worked at the Ipswich and Sandy Gallop Asylums in Queensland before opening his own private hospital in Chinchilla. He died aged 61 and was buried in Brisbane (BDM QLD B35080d/1921 p.1522).

John Thomas Smith made a remarkable ascent from his convict background into the middle class. He became an influential and well-known figure in Melbourne's founding history. In spite of the fact that Ellen did not come from a convict background she was never quite accepted by society, an issue that will be explored in more detail in later chapters. The Smith sons, with the exception of Harrie, were very successful in their employment. The careers of John Thomas Thorold and George suggest an importance placed on education, and both were educated in England. Through property ownership, Smith was able to provide a livelihood for James and Sydney. All retained the Smith's hard won middle-class status. Only three of the six sons married and two had children. The daughters also married well, albeit young by today's standards, and retained their middle-class status establishing families of their own.

4
Architecture and Spatial Layout

This chapter examines the residence at 300 Queen Street as a brand of material culture that can provide information about class structure and society. The spatial analysis of households has made useful contributions to historical archaeology for a number of years (Glassie 1975; Kent 1990; Samson 1990; Blanton 1994; Barile and Brandon 2004). While the architecture of a building conveys status, the internal spatial arrangement orders the social relations that happen within (Hourani 1990). The examination of the architecture and spatial arrangement in this chapter is based on the architectural investigations that took place at the site in the 1980s (Nigel Lewis and Associates 1982; Scott-Virtue 1984a).

ARCHITECTURE

English Georgian architecture was an extension of the Renaissance style and had evolved over almost a century before arriving in Australia. From 1840 Georgian architecture was being replaced by newer styles and comparatively little is found outside New South Wales and Tasmania. However, Georgian architecture did continue in Australia until the 1860s and beyond largely as a result of nostalgia for what settlers remembered of their homeland (Herman 1963:30–31; King and King 1982:79; Lewis 1985:68–69).

Georgian ideology emphasised order and control (Matthews 2010:59), and Georgian architecture is characterised by symmetry, restraint and minimal ornamentation. In Australia:

> There was a fortunate conjunction of the Georgian fashion in architecture and the resources of the colony. Here was simplicity, line, proportion, with a minimum of ornamentation. There was nothing wasteful about these Georgian buildings. They fulfilled their function with dignity. They could be satisfactorily executed in the material to hand. The colony and the individual could afford them. (Barnard 1963:14)

This minimal ornamentation carried a certain dignity and middle-class gentility.

All Georgian architecture was symmetrical and domestic buildings required three or five windows. This odd number of windows allowed for a symmetrical, central entrance. All other features – chimneys, wings, verandas – were also symmetrical. Windows were divided into small sections by sash bars as only small panes of glass were in production at this time (Herman 1963:37). Shutters were popular performing a practical duty in the Australian climate.

The residence at 300 Queen Street was built in the Georgian style from brick (which was stuccoed) on a bluestone base (Scott-Virtue 1984a:4). The Georgian style and form of the building is unusual in Victoria, bearing more similarities to others in New South Wales and Tasmania (Nigel Lewis and Associates 1982:6–7). The façade is symmetrical with quoined openings and corners, and a fanlight over the door. The jointing on the stucco is finished with ruled black lines: an intentional decorative technique (Scott-Virtue 1984b:10–11). All exterior window sills are limestone, possibly imported from Tasmania (Scott-Virtue 1984a:11). The presumed appearance of the façade of the residence in its original two-storey state is shown in **Figure 14**.

The deep and widely splayed window reveals, panelled in cedar, are one of the distinguished details of the internal architecture. The windows were double hung sash windows. The panelled cedar doors of the main rooms were unusually wide at 3 feet (Nigel Lewis and Associates 1982:37, 90–106).

A second storey (third level) was added in 1858–1859 and the residence then had 12 rooms (Nigel Lewis and Associates 1982:10; PROV, VPRS 5702/P0, MCC Bourke Ward Rate Books, Unit 10, 1859).

Figure 14: Presumed appearance of the original two-storey residence, west elevation (Source: Nigel Lewis and Associates 1982:32).

The construction materials closely matched those of the original building (Scott-Virtue 1984a:9). It appears that the ground floor was also 'modernised' at this time with the removal of glazing bars and the construction of a wider and grander entrance, and the widening of the central window on the first floor. Inside, improvements dating to this time possibly included grand three-piece skirting, cornices and an archway added to the ground floor hall but rather crudely executed (Nigel Lewis and Associates 1982:33, 37). Stone steps, the same width as the new entrance, were also probably added at this time along with a paved courtyard and iron fence (Nigel Lewis and Associates 1982:33, 53). The roof, constructed as part of the 1858–1859 addition, is a timber framed M-hipped roof with slate tiles on the external slopes and corrugated iron on the internal slopes (Scott-Virtue 1984a:11). There were problems with the construction of the second floor including defects in the gutters, doors, windows and chimney which required repair in the following two years (Nigel Lewis and Associates 1982:10, 47). The extension was pretentious in character but poorly executed, and Lewis (Nigel Lewis and Associates 1982:51) suggests that this reflects on Smith, the architect and attitudes of the time. For information on changes to the building after the Smiths moved on see Nigel Lewis and Associates (1982).

SITUATION

300 Queen Street is situated along the northern boundary of Melbourne's CBD, which was initially a fashionable residential area. The Smith residence was one of Melbourne's earliest true town houses and fronted directly onto the street (Priestley 1984:26–27), with outbuildings concealed to the rear of the property. The 1855 Bibbs Map shows the residence as free-standing, with a long stable building at the rear and a small building (possibly a water closet) in the south-east corner (Nigel Lewis and Associates 1982:23). The map also suggests that there was no neighbour to the right, but a long narrow building on the neighbouring block to the left. No other maps or images could be found to shed light on the layout of buildings or neighbours during the Smiths' occupation of the residence (Nigel Lewis and Associates 1982:22–23).

The stable building constructed by 1853 had bluestone footings and may have been a solid bluestone or brick structure with a slate or paling roof (Scott-Virtue 1984a:19). The coach house listed in the 1854 rate books may have been part of the stable building or a separate building. The 1855 rate book refers to '3 stall stables, coach house and loft gig house' (PROV, VPRS 5702/P0, MCC Bourke Ward Rate Books, Units 5 and 6, 1854, 1855). It is possible that there was a garden at the rear of the property while the Smiths were in residence, but there is no historical evidence for this (Nigel Lewis and Associates 1982:53).

INTERIOR LAYOUT

The original residence, completed by 1851, had eight rooms and four cellars. The interior layout of the original residence was spread over two levels plus a basement. The ground floor originally had two large rooms at the front, two smaller rooms at the back, a central passage and staircase at the rear. The first floor mirrored the ground floor with the addition of a small room filling the central space created by the hall below. This equals the eight rooms described in the rate books, but with the addition of the small room on the first floor (PROV, VPRS 5702/P0, MCC Bourke Ward Rate Books, 1849–1856). This small room may have in fact been a linen, or other, store room not counted in the rate books. The four basements followed the layout of the ground floor above.

As no plan exists of the room uses for 300 Queen Street in this era it is necessary to turn to other similar dwellings for an insight into the interior layout. Franklin House, built in 1838, is a late Georgian dwelling of similar size to 300 Queen Street with two main storeys and the classic five window façade. The original advertisement for the property described the ground floor as comprising a hall, two front parlours with marble fireplaces, and two back parlours or bedrooms. The first floor was advertised as having a dining room the full length of the house, which could be partitioned into three rooms, and two bedrooms at the back. Later use of Franklin House has the dining room and drawing room as the front two rooms on ground level. The back rooms were the study and the morning room. The large upstairs room was used as a reception room and the remaining rooms on the first floor as bedrooms. The kitchen and servant quarters were located in outbuildings. The layout was arranged around a central hall with a stairway at the rear. The remaining fireplaces were all of cedar (King and King 1982:74–79).

Room plans from other Georgian houses in Australia and America suggest that the front two rooms on the ground level were generally the dining room and drawing room either side of a hall. The two rooms at the rear of the ground level could be the sitting room, library or bedroom. Kitchens, service rooms and associated store rooms were generally attached or separate at the rear of the property, or in basements. Only occasionally the kitchen was situated within the house, on the ground floor. The first level usually comprised bedrooms exclusively. Servants' bedrooms were either situated in small rooms on the first level or in outbuildings (Architects' Emergency Committee 1970; Broadbent 1995:54; Carlin 2000:94–95).

Ground Floor

The ground floor at 300 Queen Street originally had four rooms running off a central hall (**Figure

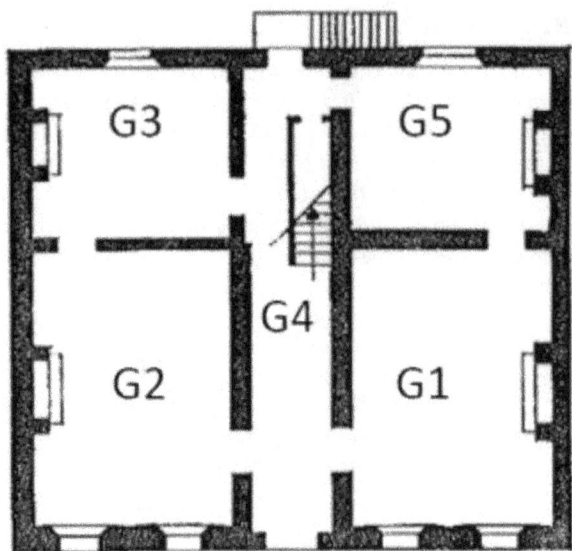

Figure 15: Ground floor plan, 1849 (Source: Scott-Virtue 1984a:23).

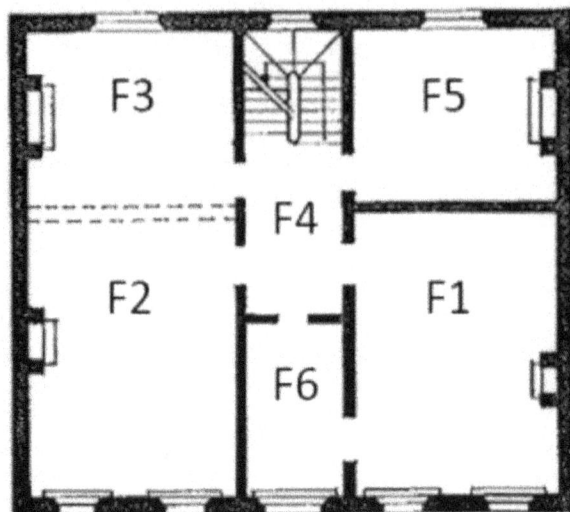

Figure 16: First floor plan, 1849 (Source: Scott-Virtue 1984a:23).

15). Rooms G1 and G2 were most likely used as a drawing room and dining room, while rooms G3 and G5 may have been a sitting room, or library, and bedroom. Jack joists to the floor at the rear of the hall suggest that there was an external balcony cantilevered at ground floor level as part of the original construction (Scott-Virtue 1984a:15). The original doorway between rooms G2 and G3 was bricked in, possibly as part of the 1858–1859 work (Scott-Virtue 1984a:15).

There was a fireplace in each ground floor room, but as they have been removed their form and material are unknown (Nigel Lewis and Associates 1982:71). The flooring on the ground floor was originally baltic pine or oregon. Staining on the floor in room G1 suggests that a square carpet inside stained borders was used in this room at some point (Scott-Virtue 1984a:15). Evidence suggests that the first wall treatment in the hall was a distemper paint, which was later replaced with plain, ashlar pattern wallpaper of a ruled design in red, simulating a masonry appearance. This style of wallpaper was used in Sydney in the 1830s and 1840s and is unusual in Victoria (Nigel Lewis and Associates 1982:59; Scott-Virtue 1984a).

First Floor

It appears that the first floor followed the same floor plan as the ground floor below (**Figure 16**). Nigel Lewis and Associates argued that the northern side of the first floor was one large room as evidenced by the continuation of the cornice and skirting, and that a partition wall was added to convert this into two rooms around 1880 (Nigel Lewis and Associates 1982:61). However, upon removal of the partition wall, investigations by Scott-Virtue (1984a:17) revealed evidence that an earlier wall had existed.

Disturbance to the wall surface and cornice 300 mm to the east of the partition wall suggest that a wall may have existed in this position, which is directly above the wall on the ground floor. This is further supported by the fact that there were two original doorways from F4 within a metre of each other and two fireplaces. It is likely that the original wall was removed to create one large room, and then the partition wall installed at a later date to re-divide it into two rooms.

It is likely that the upstairs rooms were all bedrooms. The small central room, F6, had skirting boards like the remainder of the upstairs but no fireplace (Nigel Lewis and Associates 1982:81). This may have been a small servant's bedroom.

Rooms F1, F2 had original fireplaces while the fireplace in room F5 may not have been original (Nigel Lewis and Associates 1982:78). Some walls on the first floor had bead edged lining boards (Nigel Lewis and Associates 1982:76–81).

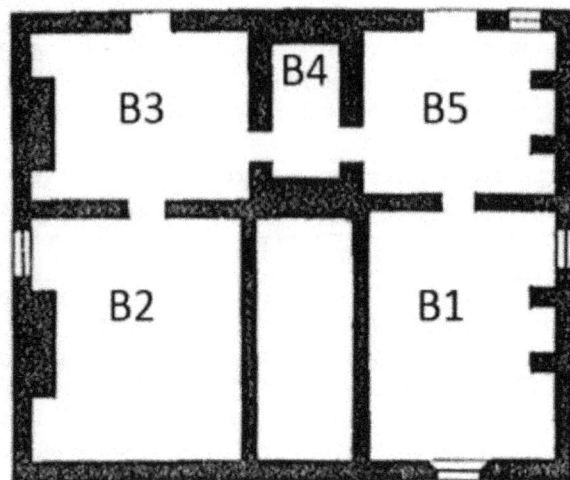

Figure 17: Basement plan, 1849 (Source: Scott-Virtue 1984a:23).

Basement

As with the first floor, the basement follows the room layout of the ground floor (**Figure 17**). The basement originally had slate floors, brick and bluestone walls, and a lath and plaster ceiling. The walls in room B1 were whitewashed, then wallpapered and later plastered over, though the timing of these treatments is unknown. The other rooms in the basement had whitewashed walls. Rooms B1 and B5 had fireplaces (Nigel Lewis and Associates 1982:57, 66, 70). The original construction included an external staircase at the rear of the residence to give access to the basement (Scott-Virtue 1984a:13).

The basement space under the hallway was accessible via a hatch in the hall floor. The earth floor in this area was not excavated down to the level of the remainder of the basement and it appears that it was not used for habitation. During archaeological investigations elaborately decorated linoleum, a bottle, builders' rubble and the remainder of a bell pull system to the front door were recovered (Scott-Virtue 1984a:13).

The presence of the bell pull system and decorated linoleum in the basement space may suggest that the basement functioned as a service area. The whitewash wall treatment and slate floors would be suitable for this purpose and the presence of fireplaces suggests that rooms B1 and B5 functioned as more than storage. The kitchen may well have been situated in the basement.

Second Floor Addition

The second floor, added in 1858–1859, has seven rooms running off a wide transverse hall (**Figure 18**). Rooms S1 and S2 had fireplaces and it is possible that room S7 was a bathroom (Scott-Virtue 1984a:18, 24). This layout, which differed to the first floor, created structural problems (Nigel Lewis and Associates 1982:37). The stairs were extended up from the first floor in the same materials and style.

Fittings and Finishes

The majority of the original fittings, such as door and window hardware, ceiling ornamentation and other finishes, were no longer present when the 1980s investigations were carried out (Nigel Lewis and Associates 1982:47). Remaining fittings included cast iron wall vents in some rooms which may be original, and ceiling roses in rooms G1, G2, G4 which probably date to the 1858–1859 improvements (Nigel Lewis and Associates 1982:71). The mixture of cedar and oregon for the original simple profile skirtings suggests that the joinery was painted, not varnished. New, more

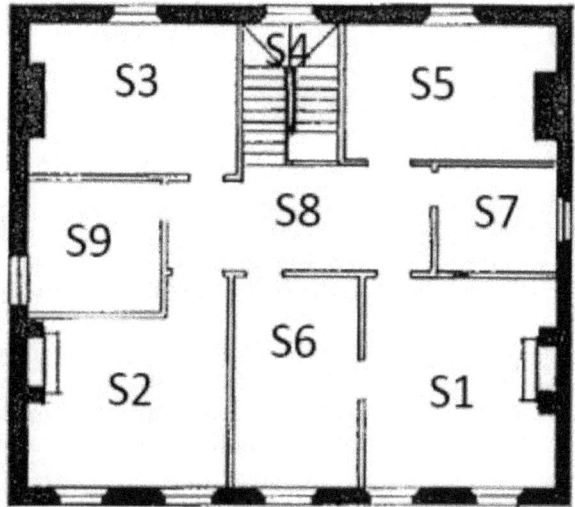

Figure 18: Second floor plan, 1859 (Source: Scott-Virtue 1984a:23).

elaborate skirtings and cornices were possibly added as part of the 1858–1859 work (Nigel Lewis and Associates 1982:55, 59).

Fireplaces had been removed from the building prior to the archaeological work in the 1980s and no photographs survive (Nigel Lewis and Associates 1982:39). It is possible that the fireplaces were in the classic simple Georgian style as at Franklin House, with marble surrounds in the front two ground floor rooms and timber elsewhere.

Evidence of a servant bell pull system was identified throughout the house including remains of the bell pull system to the front door found in the basement space below the hall (Scott-Virtue 1984a:13). This suggests that at some point the basement functioned as the main service area of the house. Throughout the remainder of the house the mechanical bell system included bell handles on either side of the main chimney breasts (Scott-Virtue 1984a:22). A zinc bell pull conduit beside the fireplace was identified in room G1 (Scott-Virtue 1984a:15). Copper wire and brass mounting from the bell pull system was also found in room S5 on the second floor indicating that the bell pull system was extended to the second floor addition (Scott-Virtue 1984a:18).

300 Queen Street had certain grandeur, and as one of the earliest true street frontage town houses in Melbourne was a significant landmark in a fashionable area at the time the Smiths were in residence. Inside, the total of eight, later extended to 12 rooms, and basement allowed for purpose-specific rooms to serve different functions, with hallways for movement between them. The rooms were laid out to facilitate and structure daily happenings including private family time, recreation, rest, receiving visitors and servants' work. This will be discussed in more detail in Chapter 6.

5
Artefacts

In order to interpret the use of material culture by the Smith family, it is first necessary to quantify and describe the artefacts from the Queen Street site. This detailed description of artefacts is a vital precursor to interpreting the assemblage (Crook et al. 2002:28). This chapter commences with a discussion and justification of the selection of the lower cesspit deposit as the focus for research. The formation of the cesspit deposit in a clear-out event is then discussed before moving on to the cataloguing methods employed in the project. The remainder of the chapter involves a full description of the domestic assemblage recovered from the cesspit grouped in six areas: about the house, eating and drinking, about the person, health and hygiene, recreation, and work. The chapter concludes with a discussion about the provenance of the artefacts.

THE LOWER CESSPIT DEPOSIT

Prior to working with the artefacts it was important to identify deposits of interest at the site. Heritage Victoria, Museum Victoria and the original excavators were contacted in order to locate the site records (such as trench books, context sheets etc.); however, they could not be found. The only available details of the site are those recorded in the reports (Nigel Lewis and Associates 1982; Scott-Virtue 1984b, 1984a). While the reports included details of areas, trenches and squares excavated (Scott-Virtue 1984b:41–52), there is no list of contexts. Some slides of the excavations were provided by Scott-Virtue, but are of limited use in reconstructing contextual information.

Many of the artefacts had area, trench (or pit) and context information (represented as A1-3/10)

to which there is no reference in the report bar inclusion in tables summarising the artefacts. Some artefacts were stored in boxes or bags with the general location recorded, and from these, elements of the site could be reconstructed. Other artefacts are unprovenanced with no way of knowing whether they came from the Smiths' residence, Smith's stables or Munro's warehouse, and therefore have very little research value.

It is not clear from the report which context numbers were from upper and which from lower deposits; however, many box and artefact labels associated the context with either the lower deposit or the upper deposit. Using this method, a series of contexts could be associated with the lower deposit (**Table 1**).

The association of contexts using the artefact labelling was more complex for the upper cesspit deposit as this deposit possibly spread across a number of squares. There is also some indication in the report that there were two distinct cultural deposits in this area (Scott-Virtue 1984b:32), but there is no information that can be used to distinguish these deposits. Square 2 was located to the north of Square 3 at the western corner (see **Figure 7**) and contained the bulk of the cultural material in the area, with part of this deposit extending into Square 4 to the east (between Squares 1 and 2). In these squares, the cultural deposit was resting directly over natural deposits. There was no trace of the upper deposit in Square 1, which was located to the north of Square 3 at the eastern corner. 'Extended Trench X' was excavated to fill the gap between Square 3 and Squares 1, 2 and 4. In addition, a plan in the report (Scott-Virtue 1984b:30) has an area north of Squares 2 and 4 labelled 'Extended

Table 1: Summary of area 1 lower cesspit contexts.

Location	Context	Context Type 1	Context Type 2	Description
Cesspit – Lower	3/0	Deposit	Refuse pit	Object from this context found with a label reading 'Final Removal of Cistern'
Cesspit – Lower	3/10	Deposit	Refuse pit	Object from this context found with a label reading 'Lower Level Deposit, Cistern'
Cesspit – Lower	3/11	Deposit	Refuse pit	Objects from this context found in a box labelled 'Lower Deposit'
Cesspit – Lower	3/8	Deposit	Refuse pit	Fragment found conjoining with 3/0 in a box labelled 'Lower Deposit'
Cesspit – Lower	3/9	Deposit	Refuse pit	Objects from this context found in a box labelled 'Lower Deposit'

4 & 5' where artefacts were also recovered (Scott-Virtue 1984b:90). As the upper deposit extends from Square 3 into Squares 2 and 4, presumably artefacts recovered from 'Extended Trench X' also belong to the upper deposit. Scott-Virtue (1984b:63) argued that the upper deposit predominantly contained material that appeared to be associated with the later use of the site as government offices, mixed with some pre-1850–1860s and Munro occupation material (Scott-Virtue 1984a:26).

The lower cesspit deposit is the most valuable deposit on the 300 Queen Street site as it represents a stratified, intact deposit of artefacts that relate to the Smith family's occupation of the site. In addition, reconstruction of site information from the artefact and box labelling has allowed artefacts from the lower cesspit deposit to be associated with integrity to that deposit. This deposit will be the focus of this monograph. The difficulty in reconstructing the location of contexts from the upper deposit along with the mixed nature of the deposit meant that it was not prioritised for this project. Further, while working with the assemblage, no artefacts could be identified as having been recovered from within the house.

CESSPIT DEPOSIT FORMATION

Artefact dating supports the argument that the lower cesspit deposit is associated with the Smith family. Of the Queen Street assemblage, 64 percent could be dated with start dates falling between 1708 and 1860, and end dates falling between 1830 and 1967 (**Table 2**). Only three artefacts fell outside the Smith phase of occupation, all of which pre-dated the phase and are still likely to be associated with the Smiths.

The lower deposit of cultural material in the cesspit had little rubble or soil within it, implying that the deposition of artefacts occurred over a short period of time and while most of the artefacts in the lower deposit were broken, a large proportion could be conjoined to form complete or near complete vessels (Scott-Virtue 1984b:46, 55). It is important to note that the artefacts recovered from the lower deposit of the cesspit do not represent the entirety of what the Smith family owned and used, or for that matter, discarded, as the deposit appears to have been formed over a short period of time. Instead, the artefacts represent things that were broken, no longer needed or out of fashion, and consequently discarded over a particular short period of time (see Schiffer 1987:47–50). Further, expensive goods that retain their value, such as best sets, silverware, or valuable jewellery, would not be discarded but kept in the family or sold second-hand (Spencer-Wood 1987:14), and cutlery, metal tools and other degradable items, though discarded, may have degraded beyond the point of identification. Yet the artefacts do constitute a sample of what the Smith family used and discarded.

Table 2: Summary of date ranges by phase.

Date From	Date To	MNI	Quantity
Pre-Smith			
1760	1830	1	5
1818	1846	2	15
Total		3	20
Smith			
1708		0	1
1720	1870	1	1
1750	1870	2	2
1750	1920	5	9
1784		1	1
1790	1850	1	9
1794		9	52
1805		48	291
1809	1920	8	8
1820		5	40
1820	1870	13	19
1820	1920	15	41
1821	1920	3	6
1825		5	36
1828		11	41
1830		2	15
1833	1847	2	12
1835		45	161
1835	1847	1	20
1835	1853	3	16
1840		4	4
1840	1870	6	9
1840	1920	8	42
1842	1867	1	21
1842	1883	1	21
1843	1883	1	2
1845	1870	1	1
1846	1967	2	2
1847	1867	3	24
1850	1920	2	20
1852		1	14
1855	1920	1	1
1859	1928	0	1
	1870	8	75
	1920	17	381
Total		236	1399
Munro			
Total		0	0
No date		132	328
Total		371	1747

Cataloguing Methods

The cataloguing methods for this project are a continuation of those developed for the project *A Historical Archaeology of the Commonweath Block 1850–1950* (Hayes 2011a:20–21). As no prior catalogue existed for the 300 Queen Street assemblage, cataloguing was conducted from scratch in the *Exploring the Archaeology of the Modern City* (EAMC) database. This database, also used for the *Commonwealth Block* project, is a custom-designed relational Microsoft Access database which was developed as part of the EAMC project (Crook et al. 2003:5, 2005). The database incorporates artefacts, contexts and type series alongside historical documentation linking people to historical place (Crook et al. 2006a, 2006b; Crook and Murray 2006:5). The EAMC database holds artefact data consolidated and generated by both the EAMC and *Commonwealth Block* projects. By cataloguing the 300 Queen Street assemblage into this database, a level of consistency will be achieved with the previously recorded data. Activities, functions, sub-functions and materials were allocated following EAMC terminology.

All domestic artefacts from the lower cesspit deposit were catalogued with the exception of some leather artefacts which had become mouldy in storage and would require time-consuming treatment by conservators before they could be handled. Building materials, industrial artefacts, and unidentifiable metal were not fully catalogued. For these records, only box location, object barcode, integrity, percent complete, activity, function, sub-function and material were recorded. No type series or MNI was created for these records.

Following the cataloguing methods established for the *Commonwealth Block* project, a range of tools for analysis were included in the cataloguing including MNIs, conjoins, type series and matching sets analysis (see Hayes 2011a:20–21; 2011c:65–70 for further details). The importance of recording such details has long been advocated (e.g. Miller 1986; Birmingham 1990:19; Wall 1992; Fitts 1999; Sussman 2000; Crook et al. 2002; Casey 2005; Crook et al. 2005) and is an essential part of cataloguing and analysis.

The Assemblage

A total of 1,747 artefact fragments representing a minimum number of 371 domestic artefacts were catalogued from the lower cesspit deposit. A further 1,088 artefact fragments that related to architecture or diet, or were unidentifiable, were catalogued but have not been included in the analysis. The largest broad material group was ceramic with 187 artefacts (838 fragments), followed by glass with 145 artefacts (809 fragments). Lithic, metal, organic, synthetic, wood and composite groups had only a small number of artefacts each (**Table 3**). The largest

Table 3: Summary of materials.

Class	Material	MNI	Quantity
Ceramic	Bone china	14	86
	Clay	1	1
	Coarse earthenware	2	2
	Dyed-body ware	4	39
	Kaolin	18	27
	Porcelain	8	18
	Prosser	4	4
	Red earthenware	2	4
	Stoneware	27	39
	Whiteware	105	603
	Yellowware	2	15
Total		*187*	*838*
Composite		8	16
Total		*8*	*16*
Glass	Glass	145	809
Total		*145*	*809*
Lithic	Slate	7	8
Total		*7*	*8*
Metal	Copper alloy	2	12
	Galvanised Iron	1	1
	Iron alloy	1	2
	Lead	3	5
	Unidentified metal	2	2
Total		*9*	*22*
Organic	Bone	7	25
	Cork	2	2
	Wax	1	19
	Wood	2	2
Total		*12*	*48*
Synthetic	Plastic	1	1
Total		*1*	*1*
Textile	Fabric	1	2
Total		*1*	*2*
Wood	Wood	1	3
Total		*1*	*3*
Total		*371*	*1747*

activity groupings were tea service, food service and beverage storage (**Table 4**). All quantities given are minimum numbers unless stated otherwise.

About the House

Artefacts from three activity groupings – domestic, collectibles/decorative and garden – were related to life about the house.

Table 4: Activity group numbers including confident and possible activity attributions.

Activity	Confident	Possible	Total MNI	Quantity	Percentage
Agricultural/Pastoral	1		1	1	0.1
Beverage service	30	3	33	125	7.2
Beverage storage	56	2	58	496	28.4
Clerical	9		9	12	0.7
Clothing	7	1	8	9	0.5
Collectibles/Decorative	2	4	6	27	1.5
Domestic	8	3	11	43	2.5
Food preparation		4	4	17	1.0
Food service	54	6	60	389	22.3
Food storage	9	3	12	17	1.0
Food/Beverage storage	4	3	7	75	4.3
Food/Tea service	1	7	8	29	1.7
Garden	2	2	4	6	0.3
Hygiene	7	3	10	104	6.0
Jewellery	2		2	2	0.1
Personal	17	2	19	28	1.6
Pharmaceutical	25	6	31	76	4.4
Recreation	29	12	41	53	3.0
Sewing	3	1	4	19	1.1
Social/Political	1		1	19	1.1
Tea service	30	3	33	172	9.8
Unidentified	9		9	28	1.6
Total	*306*	*65*	*371*	*1747*	*100.0*

Domestic

A minimum number of 11 artefacts belonged to the domestic activity group, with the majority relating to lighting (**Table 5**). A 90 percent complete bulged glass lamp chimney was found along with 40 percent of a thin glass rim which appeared to be a second lamp chimney. Bulged lamp chimneys can be dated from 1784 (Woodhead et al. 1984:58). In addition, there were two glass candlestick holder inserts: one was moulded, had a ribbed pattern and 'I A' embossed on the base, and the second was hexagonal with a pressed stepped shoulder and beading. A rectangular chandelier drop was also recovered. The items not related to lighting were two stoneware blacking bottles used for leather polish, shoe polish or stove blacking (Davies 2004:232), and two cylindrical wood handles with iron alloy through the centre that appear to be bucket handles.

Table 5: Summary of domestic artefacts.

Activity	Function	Sub-function	Material	Decoration	MNI	Fragments
Domestic	Bottle	Blacking	Stoneware	Salt glaze	2	3
	Lighting	Candlestick holder	Glass	Moulded	1	1
	Lighting	Candlestick holder	Glass	Pressed	1	1
	Lighting	Chandelier drop	Glass		1	1
	Lighting	Lamp glass	Glass	None present	1	3
	Lighting	Lamp glass	Glass	Unadorned	2	31
Domestic?	Bucket handle?	Unidentified	Composite		2	2
	Lighting?	Lamp glass?	Glass	None present	1	1
Total					*11*	*43*

Collectibles/Decorative

Two figurines were the only items confidently ascribed to the collectibles/decorative activity group. One was a moulded and hand-painted figurine of a chicken and the other was a fragment from an unidentified figurine. Further, a moulded vessel with floral hand-painted decoration, a blue dyed-body ware moulded jug depicting cherubs and two small panes of glass were possibly decorative items.

Garden

Three artefacts belonged to the garden category: a red earthenware flower pot, a coarse earthenware flower pot and what appears to be a watering can handle made from galvanised iron with banded detail. A fourth item, a whiteware vessel, may have also been a flower pot.

EATING AND DRINKING

As with many domestic archaeological assemblages, eating and drinking artefacts dominated. Of the lower cesspit assemblage, 52 percent was related to

eating and drinking: food, tea and beverage service, food and beverage storage, and food preparation.

Food Service

The vast majority (92 percent) of the 60 food service artefacts were ceramic tableware and teaware with only a small number of glass tableware and cutlery items (**Table 6**). In the ceramic tableware, only two material types were identified: whiteware (89 percent) and bone china (11 percent). Plates were the most common vessel form but there was also a range of purpose-specific vessel forms including egg cups, dishes, platters and tureens (**Figure 19**). Six different decorative techniques were identified, often combined on one vessel (**Table 7**).

Transfer-printed vessels represented 38 percent of the ceramic tableware, but interestingly multiple decorations represented 40 percent of the total. Many of these were elaborate and from the more expensive range of ceramics available (**Figure 20, Plate 1**). It is unusual for a domestic Australian food service assemblage to not be dominated by transfer prints. The next most frequent decoration was flow transfer-printed at 11 percent.

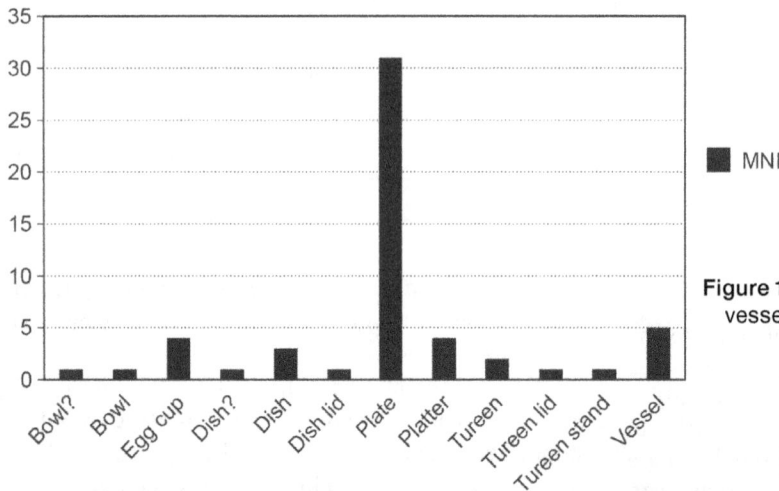

Figure 19: Summary of ceramic tableware vessel forms.

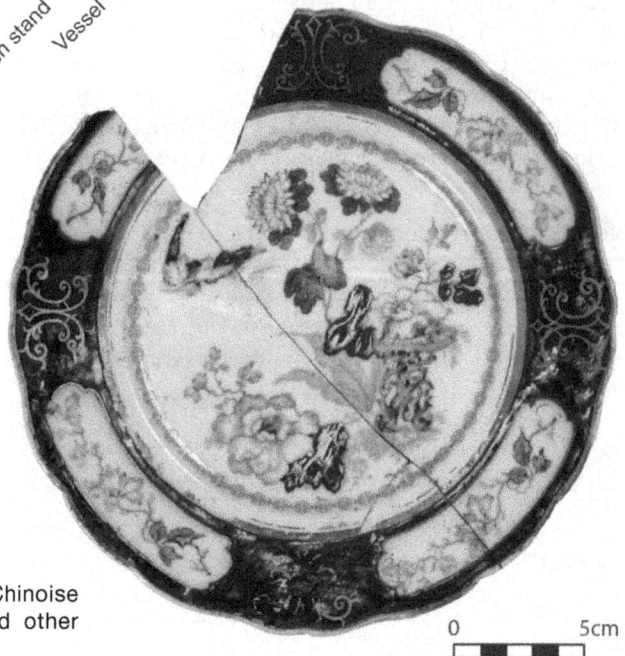

Figure 20: Transfer-printed and hand-painted Chinoise pattern plate (HA1651 – note glaze run and other flaws), see also Plate 1.

Table 6: Summary of food service artefacts.

Activity	Function	Sub-function	Class	Material	Decoration	MNI	Fragments
Food service	Plate	Muffin	Ceramic	Bone china	Moulded and gilt	1	2
	Platter	Medium	Ceramic	Bone china	Moulded and gilt	1	22
	Plate	Twiffler	Ceramic	Bone china	Moulded and sprigged	1	13
	Cup	Egg	Ceramic	Bone china	None present	2	2
	Plate	Unidentified	Ceramic	Bone china	Transfer-printed, overglaze	1	5
	Dish lid	Butter?	Ceramic	Whiteware	Flow hand-painted	1	2
	Dish?	Butter?	Ceramic	Whiteware	Flow hand-painted	1	1
	Plate	Dinner	Ceramic	Whiteware	Flow hand-painted, hand-painted and gilt	1	9
	Plate	Supper	Ceramic	Whiteware	Flow hand-painted, hand-painted and gilt	2	12
	Platter	Large	Ceramic	Whiteware	Flow hand-painted, hand-painted and gilt	1	2
	Tureen	Vegetable	Ceramic	Whiteware	Flow hand-painted, hand-painted and gilt	1	13
	Plate	Twiffler	Ceramic	Whiteware	Flow transfer	4	41
	Tureen lid	Unidentified	Ceramic	Whiteware	Flow transfer	1	8
	Tureen stand	Unidentified	Ceramic	Whiteware	Flow transfer	1	2
	Plate	Twiffler	Ceramic	Whiteware	Flow transfer and gilt	2	15
	Cup	Egg	Ceramic	Whiteware	Flow transfer and hand-painted	2	7
	Plate	Twiffler	Ceramic	Whiteware	Hand-painted and lustre	1	9
	Bowl	Medium	Ceramic	Whiteware	Transfer-printed	1	17
	Bowl?	Medium	Ceramic	Whiteware	Transfer-printed	1	1
	Dish	Serving	Ceramic	Whiteware	Transfer-printed	2	21
	Plate	Large	Ceramic	Whiteware	Transfer-printed	2	19
	Plate	Supper	Ceramic	Whiteware	Transfer-printed	2	10
	Plate	Twiffler	Ceramic	Whiteware	Transfer-printed	1	1
	Plate	Unidentified	Ceramic	Whiteware	Transfer-printed	4	9
	Platter	Large	Ceramic	Whiteware	Transfer-printed	1	20
	Platter	Small	Ceramic	Whiteware	Transfer-printed	1	11
	Tureen	Soup	Ceramic	Whiteware	Transfer-printed	1	6
	Vessel	Unidentified	Ceramic	Whiteware	Transfer-printed	1	1
	Dish	Vegetable	Ceramic	Whiteware	Transfer-printed and hand-painted	1	7
	Plate	Dinner	Ceramic	Whiteware	Transfer-printed and hand-painted	2	22
	Plate	Large	Ceramic	Whiteware	Transfer-printed and hand-painted	1	11
	Plate	Soup	Ceramic	Whiteware	Transfer-printed and hand-painted	4	43
	Plate	Supper	Ceramic	Whiteware	Transfer-printed and hand-painted	1	3
	Plate	Unidentified	Ceramic	Whiteware	Transfer-printed and hand-painted	1	2
	Vessel	Unidentified	Ceramic	Whiteware	Transfer-printed and hand-painted	1	1
	Cutlery	Knife?	Composite	Wood and metal		1	2
	Vessel	Unidentified	Glass	Glass	Cut		1
	Dish	Salt?	Glass	Glass	Moulded	1	1
Food service?	Vessel	Unidentified	Ceramic	Whiteware	Transfer-printed	3	7
	Cutlery?	Knife?	Composite	Wood and metal		1	1
	Dish	Unidentified	Glass	Glass	Cut	1	2
	Vessel	Unidentified	Glass	Glass	Cut	1	5
Total						60	389

Table 7: Summary of decorations on ceramic food service vessels (positively identified pattern names are in bold).

Decoration	Pattern	MNI	Fragments
Flow hand-painted	Geometric	1	2
Flow hand-painted	Unidentified	1	1
Total Flow hand-painted		*2*	*3*
Flow transfer	**Alpine**	4	28
Flow transfer	Floral	1	2
Flow transfer	**Pelew**	1	21
Total Flow transfer		*6*	*51*
Moulded and gilt	Banded	1	2
Total Gilt		*1*	*2*
Moulded and sprigged	Grape vine	1	13
Total Sprigged		*1*	*13*
Transfer-printed	**Aesop's fables**	1	17
Transfer-printed	**Albion**	1	20
Transfer-printed	**Asiatic pheasants**	3	9
Transfer-printed	**British flowers**	1	11
Transfer-printed	Chinese scene	1	10
Transfer-printed	Floral	2	15
Transfer-printed	Geometric	1	1
Transfer-printed	Scenic	1	3
Transfer-printed	**Two temples**	1	3
Transfer-printed	Unidentified	1	1
Transfer-printed	**Willow**	7	33
Transfer-printed, overglaze	Chinoise	1	5
Total Transfer-printed		*21*	*128*
Flow hand-painted, hand-painted and gilt	Chinoise	5	36
Flow transfer and gilt	**Dagger border**	2	15
Flow transfer and hand-painted	Floral	2	7
Hand-painted and lustre	Floral	1	9
Moulded and gilt	Scroll, floral	1	22
Transfer-printed and hand-painted	Chinese flowers	9	75
Transfer-printed and hand-painted	Chinoise	1	3
Transfer-printed and hand-painted	Floral	1	11
Total Multiple decorations		*22*	*178*
None present		2	2
Total		*55*	*377*

The vessels that included transfer-printed designs were predominantly in blue with 84 percent of the total. Blue was the most frequently produced and cheapest transfer colour; however, other colours were available from 1828 (Brooks 2005:72). It is unusual for other colours to be represented in such small numbers: four black, one grey and one red overglaze. Similarly, of the 18 vessels that included flow transfer-printed designs, 17 were blue and one black. Of the printed patterns, including standard prints, flow prints and those with additional highlights the most common patterns were Chinese themed, floral and scenic patterns.

There were nine matching sets with 64 percent of all the ceramic tableware vessels being part of a set (**Table 8**). Two types of sets were recorded: 1) actual matching sets were determined by identical pattern or presence of a makers mark, and 2) complementary sets were made up of common patterns but not of identical patterns. Each of the sets comprised

Table 8: Summary of matching tableware sets.

Matching Set ID	Matching Set Type	Function	Decoration	Pattern	MNI	Fragments
1615	Complementary common	Platter	Moulded and gilt	Scroll, floral	1	22
	Complementary common	Plate	Moulded and gilt	Banded	1	2
Total 1615					2	24
1626	Complementary common	Plate	Moulded and sprigged	Grape vine	1	13
Total 1626					1	13
1635	Actual match	Plate	Flow hand-painted, hand-painted and gilt	Chinoise	3	21
	Actual match	Platter	Flow hand-painted, hand-painted and gilt	Chinoise	1	2
	Actual match	Tureen	Flow hand-painted, hand-painted and gilt	Chinoise	1	13
Total 1635					5	36
1639	Actual match	Dish	Transfer-printed and hand-painted	Chinese flowers	1	7
	Actual match	Plate	Transfer-printed and hand-painted	Chinese flowers	7	67
	Actual match	Vessel	Transfer-printed and hand-painted	Chinese flowers	1	1
Total 1639					9	75
1649	Actual match	Plate	Flow transfer and gilt	Dagger border	2	15
Total 1649					2	15
1679	Complementary common	Plate	Transfer-printed	Asiatic pheasants	2	8
	Complementary common	Vessel	Transfer-printed	Asiatic pheasants	1	1
Total 1679					3	9
1687	Complementary common	Dish	Transfer-printed	Willow	2	21
	Complementary common	Plate	Transfer-printed	Willow	4	11
	Complementary common	Vessel	Transfer-printed	Willow	1	1
Total 1687					7	33
1713	Actual match	Plate	Flow transfer	Alpine	3	20
	Actual match	Tureen lid	Flow transfer	Alpine	1	8
Total 1713					4	28
1724	Actual match	Egg cup	Flow transfer and hand-painted	Floral	2	7
Total 1724					2	7
Total					35	240

only small numbers of vessels, but they may have originally been part of a complete set. The largest actual matching set was the transfer-printed and hand-painted Chinese flowers pattern comprising soup plates, dinner plates and a vegetable dish (**Figure 21, Plate 2**). Being transfer-printed with hand-painted highlights, this set would have been relatively more expensive than a straight transfer-print design (see Allison and Cremin 2006:61). Another large set was the 'Alpine' pattern with three plates and one tureen lid, and five tea service vessels (**Figure 22, Plate 3** see section below on tea service). The gilded and sprigged food service vessels may have been used with the teaware sets of the same decoration discussed below.

Interestingly, flaws were noted on all of the ceramic vessels: 66 percent had noticeable but not major flaws, 28 percent had minor flaws and 6 percent had major flaws. Significant savings could be made by purchasing flawed goods (Crook 2011:585).

Four makers were identified from makers' marks: Copeland and Spode, Copeland and Garrett and C. & W.K Harvey. The 'Dagger Border' pattern was designed by Enoch Wood & Sons and they are the likely maker though no maker's mark could confirm this (**Figure 23, Plate 4**). All were Staffordshire based makers, reflecting the dominance of Staffordshire potteries in the ceramic tableware market.

Figure 21: Chinese flowers plate from matching set (HA1641), see also Plate 2.

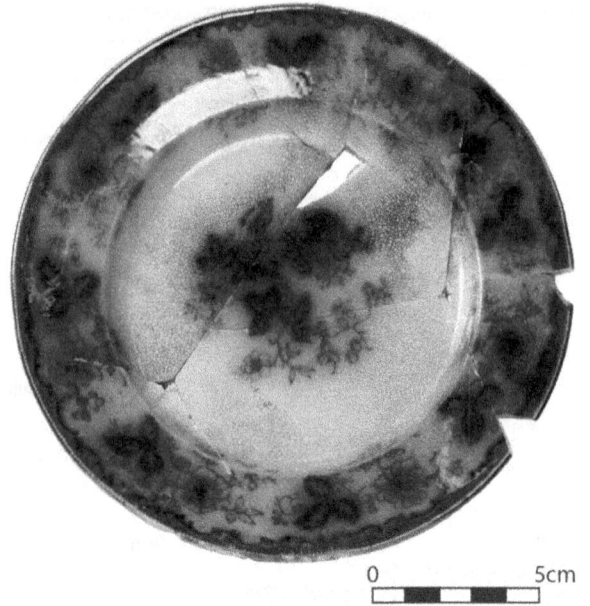

Figure 22: 'Alpine' pattern plate from matching set (HA1716.1), see also Plate 3.

Other artefacts in the food service category included cutlery and glass vessels. Cutlery is highly susceptible to rust and decay in the archaeological record, so unidentifiable rusted objects may have in fact been cutlery. Two wooden handles, most likely from knives, were the only possible cutlery items. Both had the metal tang in place inside the handle, but the blade had rusted away. It is possible that the knives were used for purposes other than food service. Three glass artefacts may have been used for food service. A heavy, shallow dish with alternating moulded panels and flutes on the body may have been a salt dish/cellar. A cut glass dish

and another cut glass floral vessel may also have been used for food service.

Tea Service

The tea service artefacts recovered from the lower cesspit were exclusively ceramic vessels: 70 percent whiteware, 24 percent bone china and 6 percent porcelain (**Table 9**). The vessel forms were dominated by tea cups with 55 percent and saucers with 33 percent. The only other definitely attributed vessel form was a tea pot lid (**Figure 24**). Five decorative techniques were identified on the tea service vessels (**Table 10**).

Figure 23: 'Dagger Border' pattern plate (HA1649), see also Plate 4.

Figure 24: Tea pot lid (HA1723).

Table 9: Summary of tea service artefacts.

Activity	Function	Sub-function	Material	Decoration	MNI	Fragments
Tea service	Cup	Tea	Bone china	Gilt	2	12
	Cup	Tea	Bone china	Sprigged	1	3
	Cup	Tea	Whiteware	Flow transfer	11	62
	Cup	Tea	Whiteware	Transfer-printed	4	18
	Pot lid	Tea	Whiteware	Flow transfer	1	1
	Saucer	Tea	Bone china	Gilt	1	7
	Saucer	Tea	Bone china	Moulded and gilt	1	3
	Saucer	Tea	Bone china	Sprigged	2	13
	Saucer	Tea	Porcelain	Sprigged	1	11
	Saucer	Tea	Whiteware	Flow transfer	3	20
	Saucer	Tea	Whiteware	Transfer-printed	3	16
Tea service?	Saucer?	Tea?	Bone china	Gilt	1	1
	Saucer?	Tea?	Whiteware	Flow transfer	1	1
	Vessel	Unidentified	Bone china	Gilt		1
	Vessel	Unidentified	Bone china	None present		2
	Vessel	Unidentified	Porcelain	None present	1	1
Total					33	172

Table 10: Summary of decorations on tea service vessels (positively identified pattern names are in bold).

Decoration	Pattern	MNI	Fragments
Flow transfer	**Alpine**	5	35
	Chinese scene	7	32
	Chinoise	1	5
	Cyrene	1	7
	Floral		1
	Unidentified	2	4
Total Flow		16	84
Gilt	Banded	2	4
	Banded, tea leaf	2	17
Total Gilt		4	21
Moulded and gilt	Fluted, banded	1	3
Total Moulded and gilt		1	3
Sprigged	Floral	1	4
	Grape vine	3	23
Total Sprigged		4	27
Transfer-printed	Classical scene	1	4
	Floral	1	1
	Scenic	2	3
	Vignette	3	26
Total Transfer		7	34
None Present		1	3
Total		33	172

Interestingly, 48 percent were flow transfer-printed while only 21 percent were decorated with standard transfer prints. Smaller numbers were gilded or sprigged and one vessel featured both moulding and gilding. Of the flow transfer prints, all were blue. However, there was more variety in the standard transfer prints with four blue, two black and one red vessels. A similar preference for pattern as the food service vessels was noted: Chinese themed patterns dominated with floral and scenic vessels also in high numbers.

As with the ceramic tableware, all of the teaware vessels were flawed. Noticeable but not major flaws were noted on 64 percent, minor flaws on 30 percent and major flaws on 6 percent. Interestingly this is almost exactly the percentages noted on the food service vessels suggesting that availability and/or patterns of purchasing were consistent for both tea and tableware.

In total, 64 percent of the tea service vessels belonged to a matching set (**Table 11**). There were five matching sets: three were definite sets (as determined by their distinctive pattern or maker's mark), while two comprised similar vessels that could have functioned as sets. Each of the sets included only small numbers of vessels; however, they may have originally been part of a complete set. The 'Alpine' pattern set was the largest definite set and was the only actual matching set to also comprise food service vessels.

Makers could be identified for only two of the tea service vessels. A flow transfer tea cup decorated with a Chinese scene was marked 'Copeland/Late

Table 11: Summary of matching teaware sets.

Matching Set ID	Matching Set Type	Function	Decoration	Pattern	MNI	Fragments
1615	Complementary common	Cup	Gilt	Banded	1	2
		Cup	Gilt	Banded, tea leaf	1	10
		Saucer	Gilt	Banded	1	1
		Saucer	Gilt	Banded, tea leaf	1	7
		Saucer	Moulded and gilt	Fluted, banded	1	3
Total 1615					*5*	*23*
1626	Complementary common	Cup	Sprigged	Grape vine	1	3
		Saucer	Sprigged	Floral	1	4
		Saucer	Sprigged	Grape vine	2	20
Total 1626					*4*	*27*
1684	Actual match	Cup	Transfer-printed	Vignette	2	16
		Saucer	Transfer-printed	Vignette	1	10
Total 1684					*3*	*26*
1709	Actual match	Cup	Flow transfer	Chinese scene	3	16
		Saucer	Flow transfer	Chinese scene	1	3
Total 1709					*4*	*19*
1713	Actual match	Cup	Flow transfer	Alpine	4	26
		Saucer	Flow transfer	Alpine	1	9
Total 1713					*5*	*35*
Total					*21*	*130*

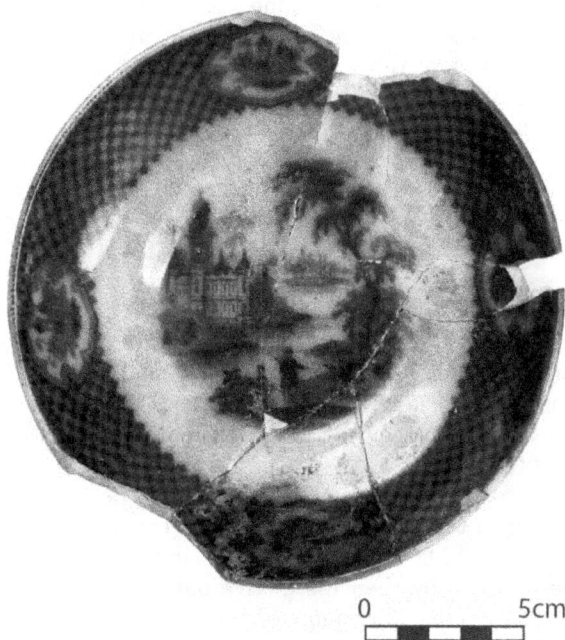

Figure 25: 'Cyrene' pattern saucer made by John and Thomas Lockett (HA1728), see also Plate 5.

Spode' and was made in Staffordshire, England between 1847 and 1867 (Godden 1964:171). A saucer with the flow transfer 'Cyrene' pattern (**Figure 25, Plate 5**) was made by John and Thomas Lockett in Staffordshire after 1835 (Williams 1978:248).

Food/Tea Service

A further 25 ceramic fragments with a MNI of nine could possibly have been from food or tea service vessels, or alternatively hygiene or decorative vessels. These were small fragments (5 or 10 percent complete) of whiteware, dyed-bodied ware and stoneware from unidentifiable vessel forms with transfer-printed, flow transfer and moulded decorations.

Beverage Service

The beverage service artefacts were predominantly drinking glasses along with a smaller number of jugs and two decanter stoppers (**Table 12**). Twenty-six drinking glasses were recovered including 16 tumblers, five wine glasses, three port/sherry glasses and two champagne glasses. As with the ceramic table and teaware, there were matching sets of drinking glasses. Five identical pressed Gothic arch tumblers formed a set. Also, a series of not identical, but complementary cut glass tumblers, wine glasses, champagne glasses, port/sherry glasses may have originally been from sets. Cut drinking glasses were superior to their pressed counterparts (Jones 2000:174). Two pressed panelled tumblers, along with two pressed panelled wine glasses may have formed a less formal set. Other tumblers were mitred, diamond facetted or had multiple decorative elements. All of these

Table 12: Summary of beverage service artefacts.

Activity	Function	Sub-function	Material	Decoration	MNI	Fragments
Beverage service	Decanter stopper	Unidentified	Glass	Unadorned	1	1
	Decanter stopper	Unidentified	Glass	Moulded	1	1
	Glass	Champagne?	Glass	Cut	2	5
	Glass	Port/sherry	Glass	Cut	3	5
	Glass	Tumbler	Glass	Cut	5	31
	Glass	Tumbler	Glass	Pressed	11	28
	Glass	Tumbler	Glass	None present		5
	Glass	Unidentified	Glass	Cut	1	9
	Glass	Unidentified	Glass	None present		2
	Glass	Unidentified	Glass	Unadorned	1	1
	Glass	Wine	Glass	Cut	2	3
	Glass	Wine	Glass	None present	1	1
	Glass	Wine	Glass	Pressed	2	6
	Glass	Tumbler?	Glass	Pressed		1
Beverage service?	Glass?	Unidentified	Glass	None present		1
	Jug	Unidentified	Dyed-body ware	Moulded	1	21
	Jug	Unidentified	Stoneware	Moulded	1	1
	Jug	Large	Whiteware	Flow transfer	1	2
	Jug	Unidentified	Whiteware	Transfer-printed		1
Total					33	125

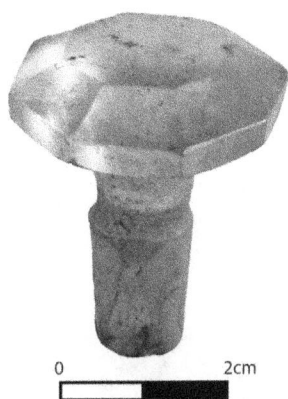

Figure 26: Panelled, mushroom decanter stopper (HA1891).

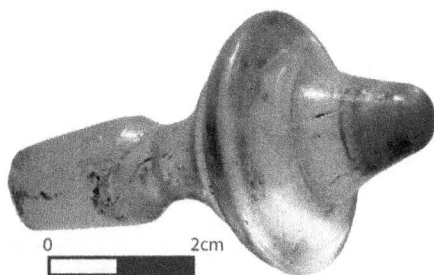

Figure 27: Decanter stopper with sloped down finial (HA1926).

Figure 28: Moulded dyed-bodied ware jug (HA1672).

patterns were common decorations for 19th-century glassware (Jones 2000:174).

Other artefacts related to beverage service were decanter stoppers and jugs. Two stoppers from spirit or sherry bottles were found (**Figure 26** and **Figure 27**). Of the four jugs, three were very fragmentary and might not be related to beverage service. The fourth was a moulded, light blue dyed-bodied ware jug with a dancing couple surrounded by foliated scrolls and fleur-de-lys (**Figure 28**). This jug may have been used for water or other liquids at the table; but it is also possible that it was used as a vase. All of the ceramic jugs had minor or moderate flaws.

Food Storage

A total of 12 vessels related to food storage including jars and bottles (**Table 13**). Three wide mouthed bung jars may have contained pickled foods such as olives, gherkins, onions or capers (**Figure 29, Plate 6**) (Lawrence 2006:79). A shoulder fragment from a fourth Bristol glazed stoneware vessel may also have been a bung jar. A rim fragment from a whiteware vessel with a cylindrical, recessed rim may have been a jam jar. Another jar was a Staffordshire mustard jar with a transfer-printed and hand-painted oriental scene (**Figure 30, Plate 7**). A fragment from a coarse earthenware vessel with a moulded pattern including thistles may have been for food storage. There were also two light green pickle bottles, a sauce bottle and a fluted salad oil/vinegar bottle. It is perhaps worth noting that no Chinese storage vessels were found.

Beverage Storage

There were 56 bottles and two corks associated with beverage storage. The sub-functions given in **Table 14** are based on the shape of the vessel and may not in fact reflect what beverage was purchased in that bottle. Bottles were extensively reused and recycled in the 19th century and were frequently

Table 13: Summary of food storage artefacts.

Activity	Function	Sub-function	Class	Material	Decoration	MNI	Fragments
Food storage	Jar	Bung	Ceramic	Stoneware	Bristol	2	3
	Jar	Bung	Ceramic	Stoneware	Bristol and Impressed	1	2
	Jar	Unidentified	Ceramic	Stoneware	Bristol and Impressed	1	1
	Jar	Mustard	Ceramic	Whiteware	Transfer-printed and hand-painted	1	1
	Bottle	Pickle	Glass	Glass		3	5
	Bottle	Pickle	Glass	Glass	Moulded		1
	Bottle	Sauce	Glass	Glass		1	1
Food storage?	Vessel	Unidentified	Ceramic	Coarse earthenware	Moulded	1	1
	Jar	Jam?	Ceramic	Whiteware	Unadorned	1	1
	Bottle	Oil/vinegar?	Glass	Glass	Moulded	1	1
Total						12	17

Figure 29: Bristol glazed stoneware bung jar (HA1570), see also Plate 6.

Figure 30: Whiteware mustard jar (HA1655), see also Plate 7.

Table 14: Summary of beverage storage artefacts.

Activity	Function	Sub-function	Class	Material	Decoration	MNI	Fragments
Beverage storage	Bottle	Aerated water	Glass	Glass		9	11
	Bottle	Beer/wine	Glass	Glass		22	117
	Bottle	Beer/wine	Glass	Glass	Moulded	1	1
	Bottle	Beer/wine?	Glass	Glass		1	1
	Bottle	Champagne	Glass	Glass		2	11
	Bottle	Champagne?	Glass	Glass		4	26
	Bottle	Gin	Glass	Glass		7	75
	Bottle	Ginger beer?	Ceramic	Stoneware	Salt glaze	2	2
	Bottle	Unidentified	Ceramic	Stoneware	Bristol	1	3
	Bottle	Unidentified	Glass	Glass		1	201
	Bottle	Unidentified	Glass	Glass		1	34
	Bottle	Wine	Glass	Glass		4	9
	Bottle cork	Beer/wine?	Organic	Cork		2	2
Beverage storage?	Bottle?	Unidentified	Ceramic	Stoneware	Salt glaze	0	2
	Bottle?	Unidentified	Glass	Glass		1	1
Total						58	496

refilled domestically, returned to manufacturers for refilling or redistributed by second hand bottle traders (Busch 1991:113–116; Woff 2014; Ellis and Woff 2017). This makes definite conclusions about what was being consumed at a site troublesome.

Based on form, alcohol bottles formed 74 percent of the beverage storage assemblage and included beer/wine, champagne (**Figure 31**), wine and gin bottles (**Figure 32**). However, the 26 bottles classified as beer/wine shape were often also used for non-alcoholic beverages. One beer/wine bottle embossed with a rearing horse and marked 'REGISTERED' was made by Tooth & Co. in Sydney after 1855. A large cream stoneware bottle may have originally

Figure 31: Champagne bottle (HA1747).

Figure 32: Case gin bottle (HA1781).

Figure 33: Dixon's Genuine aerated water bottle (HA1802).

Figure 34: J. Schweppes & Co. torpedo aerated water bottle (HA1803).

contained sprits and had an illegible maker's mark. Four beer/wine bottles and one champagne bottle still had the corks in place, and one cork was found without an associated bottle.

A number of non-alcoholic beverage bottles were also recovered, nine of which were torpedo shaped aerated water bottles, one with a cork still in place. These convex based bottles were first patented by William F. Hamilton in 1809 to ensure the bottle was stored on its side keeping the cork wet and preventing loss of carbonation (Lindsey 2011, www. sha.org/bottle). Two of the bottles were marked with the distributor: Dixon Aerated Water in Melbourne and J. Schweppes & Co. in London (**Figure 33** and **Figure 34**). In addition, two salt glazed bottle finishes were probably ginger beer bottles.

Food/Beverage Storage

A further seven vessels may have related to food or beverage storage. The vessels included salt and Bristol glazed stoneware bottles or jars, glass bottles and jars, and a light green bottle stopper with a ground shaft.

Food Preparation

Four vessels were possibly associated with food preparation. Three of these were small fragments with vessel shapes that suggest usage for food preparation. The fourth was a large yellowware open dish with a flanged rim probably for baking. The dish had a maker's mark indicating that it was made by an English pottery in Ashby-De-La-Zouch.

About the Person

A number of artefacts were used by individuals and fell into three categories: cosmetics, adornment and clothing.

Personal

Eight plain whiteware pots (four with lids, three bases and one non-matching lid) probably contained ointment or cosmetics (**Figure 35**). Two small unadorned whiteware dishes with shallow concave surfaces may have been cosmetic palettes. One palette was marked 'G*Smith' and had use-wear scratches on the surface. Two items were related to hair care: a wooden hair brush handle and a macassar oil bottle embossed with 'GENUINE/ MACASSAR OIL/ FOR THE HAIR/

Figure 35: Ointment/cosmetic pot (HA1590).

Table 15: Summary of personal items.

Activity	Function	Sub-function	Class	Material	Decoration	MNI	Fragments
Personal	Palette	Cosmetic	Ceramic	Stoneware	Unadorned	2	2
	Pot	Ointment	Ceramic	Whiteware	Unadorned	7	12
	Pot lid	Ointment	Ceramic	Whiteware	Unadorned	1	1
	Bottle	Macassar oil	Glass	Glass		1	1
	Bottle	Perfume	Glass	Glass	Cut	2	2
	Bottle	Perfume	Glass	Glass	Moulded	1	1
	Spectacle lens	Unidentified	Glass	Glass		1	1
	Brush	Unidentified	Organic	Bone		1	1
	Brush	Hair	Wood	Wood	None present	1	3
Personal?	Bottle	Unidentified	Glass	Glass		0	1
	Mirror?	Unidentified	Glass	Glass		1	1
	Handle?	Unidentified	Metal	Iron alloy		0	1
	Plate	Name	Metal	Lead	Unadorned	1	1
Clothing	Closure	Button	Ceramic	Prosser	Moulded	1	1
	Closure	Button	Ceramic	Prosser	Unadorned	3	3
	Closure	Button	Organic	Bone	Carved	1	1
	Closure	Button	Organic	Wood	Carved	1	1
	Closure	Hook and eye	Metal	Copper alloy		1	1
Clothing?	Unidentified	Unidentified	Textile	Fabric		1	2
Jewellery?	Brooch?	Brooch?	Glass	Glass	Moulded	1	1
	Decorative	Bead	Synthetic	Plastic	Unadorned	1	1
Total						29	39

LONDON'. Macassar oil was a coconut or palm oil used predominantly by men, but also by women and children, to dress the hair. A second handle may also have been from a hair brush.

Also related to personal appearance (**Table 15**) were three perfume bottles. One was moulded with large flowers and scrolls on the body, a second had cut panels on the body and neck, and alternating facets and mitres on the shoulder, and the third had cut facets on the body. The cut glass bottles represent more expensive items that may have been reused rather than purchased with the perfume inside. A mirror fragment may have come from a personal or hand mirror.

Two other somewhat unusual artefacts fell into the personal items category. The first was a rectangular lead name plate measuring 76 x 41 millimetres, hand incised with 'MARY NIHILL' on one side and 'WC' on the other. Presumably this originally functioned as a name plate to identify a possession such as a trunk or case. It is curious that the obverse is incised with 'WC' suggesting that the plate might have been repurposed to label a water closet. The second artefact was a rusted iron alloy handle, the shape of which suggests that it may have been a walking stick handle. In addition, a lens from a broken or redundant pair of spectacles was found.

Jewellery

Only two items belonged to the jewellery category: a purple glass object with D-shaped facets on the upper face and a bevelled, shaped edge may have been from a brooch.

Clothing

Five definite buttons and one possible button were the only items found that were related to clothing. Four Prosser ceramic buttons with four-hole-sew-through attachment were found: three were unadorned and one had a beaded band around the rim. The Prosser technique for button manufacture was introduced in 1840 (Sprague 2002:111). Two buttons made from organic materials were also found: one made from bone with four-hole-sew-through attachment, a circular well and carved band around the rim, and another of wood with a carved band around the rim and unidentifiable attachment type. Sew-through attachment buttons were generally more utilitarian and cheaper than shanked types (Porter and Ferrier 2004:320). The four Prosser buttons were between seven and ten millimetres in diameter suggesting that they were used for underclothing, shirts, children's clothes or women's garments. The wood and bone buttons were larger and possibly used for coats, jackets or trousers (Birmingham 1992:105; Lindbergh 1999:53–54; Sprague 2002:124). One hook and eye closure was also found.

HEALTH AND HYGIENE

Artefacts related to maintaining health and hygiene comprised 8 percent of the Queen Street assemblage.

Pharmaceutical

A total of 30 bottles and one bottle stopper were associated with pharmaceutical storage by their shape or type. Fifteen of these were small cylindrical medicine bottles (**Figure 36**). Two other bottles, one cylindrical and the other hexagonal in section, were around 40 millimetres in height and may have contained single dose medicine (**Figure 37**). A further six bottles were medium and large flat sided and panelled, three of which were light blue and almost identical in shape (**Figure 38**). Three larger cylindrical, three ovoid and one undetermined shape medicine bottles were also found. The bottle stopper, which had a flat oblong head and ground shank, was of the type associated with dispensary and druggist bottles (**Figure 39**). Only two of the medicine bottles

had embossed lettering and neither was sufficient to identify the maker. This range of medicine bottles suggests that a variety of medicines were being purchased by the Smith family.

Hygiene

Ten artefacts were related to personal hygiene, seven of which were ceramic vessels. Three chamber pots were recovered: one had a transfer-printed classical scene depicting Athena aboard a chariot (**Figure 40, Plate 8**), another a flow transfer floral pattern made by Copeland and Garrett between 1835 and 1847, and the third was an unadorned whiteware which was smaller than the average chamber pot and therefore possibly a child's. In addition, a black transfer-printed soap dish with a perforated base was recovered. Three other ceramic vessels may have been related to hygiene: a handle from a large jug and two transfer-printed fragments possibly from chamber pots. No matching sets were identified among the ceramic hygiene vessels. Moderate flaws were noted on six of the ceramic vessels and minor flaws on one. The only other artefacts used for hygiene purposes were three bone handled toothbrushes.

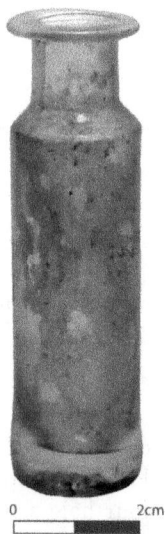

Figure 38: Flat sided light blue medicine bottle (HA1826).

Figure 37: Hexagonal single dose medicine bottle (HA1835).

Figure 36: Small, cylindrical medicine bottle (HA1833).

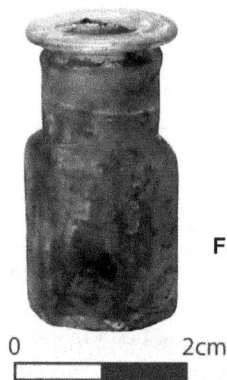

Figure 39: Apothecary type bottle stopper (HA1890).

Figure 40: Transfer-printed chamber pot (HA1657), see also Plate 8.

RECREATION

Of the 41 artefacts in the recreation category, 18 were clay pipes (**Table 16**). Half of the clay pipes were decorated: three were figurative with the bowl moulded into the shape of a human face, three had leaf motifs on the front and back of the bowl, another had a petal shape over bowl base, panelled body and scalloped rim, and another had a rouletted rim. Four of the pipes had embossed lettering indicating the type of pipe or maker. Two of the pipes were made by Duncan McDougall of Glasgow between 1846 and 1967 (Davey 1987:345). One of the McDougall pipes was a Burns Cutty shape pipe. The third marked pipe was made by T. Milo of the Strand, London. The fourth was fragmentary and the maker could not be identified, although it was also marked as a Cutty pipe. Usewear, in the form of burning of the interior bowl, was noted on 12 of the pipes.

The remaining artefacts in the recreation category were toys and game pieces. All of the 19 marbles were ceramic, and 15 of these were undecorated. A number of the redware and stoneware marbles attributed in **Table 16** with a question mark may have been baking weights rather than game pieces. Baking weights were used to hold down the base of an empty pie crust while baking. Two of these unadorned marbles were found in a small cylindrical bark case with a flat base which appeared to be a tobacco container reused to carry marbles. This suggests that whatever the intended original purpose of the marbles, they were later used by children. Four marbles were decorated and definitely game pieces. One marble had blue and green dye through the ceramic body to imitate marble, and three others had a hand-painted check pattern. An unadorned porcelain marble was also probably a game piece.

A small number of other toys were also recovered from the site: a porcelain doll's head with hand-painted black hair, pink cheeks and red mouth, a ceramic figurine with reversible happy and sad faces, a fluted whiteware plate from a doll's tea set, and a metal toy canon with a barrel and two wheels.

SEWING

Four sewing related artefacts were recovered from the cesspit including a wood lace making bobbin with carved bands and fluted, a copper alloy thimble, thread on a leather bobbin, and a possible thread reel holder made of bone and carved. A small selection of items, but they do indicate that sewing and lace making were done at Queen Street.

WORK

A small number of artefacts were related to work at 300 Queen Street, the majority of which were clerical, namely pencils and ink bottles.

Clerical

Two rectangular glass ink bottles were found in the cesspit: one with a burst off rim and another with a straight rim. Seven slate pencils were also found. Slate pencils were cheap and durable writing

Table 16: Summary of recreation artefacts.

Activity	Function	Sub-function	Class	Material	Decoration	MNI	Fragments
Recreation	Toy	Doll	Ceramic	Porcelain	Hand-painted	1	1
	Toy	Doll	Ceramic	Whiteware	Moulded and hand-painted	1	1
	Game piece	Marble	Ceramic	Porcelain	Dyed	1	1
	Game piece	Marble	Ceramic	Porcelain	Hand-painted	3	3
	Game piece	Marble	Ceramic	Porcelain	Unadorned	1	1
	Smoking	Pipe	Ceramic	Kaolin		4	5
	Smoking	Pipe	Ceramic	Kaolin	Impressed	1	1
	Smoking	Pipe	Ceramic	Kaolin	Moulded	8	9
	Smoking	Pipe	Ceramic	Kaolin	None present	2	8
	Smoking	Pipe	Ceramic	Kaolin	Unadorned	3	4
	Doll's tea set	Plate	Ceramic	Whiteware	Moulded	1	1
	Game piece	Marbles in case	Composite	Stoneware and bark		2	3
	Toy	Canon	Metal	Lead		1	3
Recreation?	Game piece?	Marble?	Ceramic	Red earthenware	Unadorned	1	1
	Game piece?	Marble?	Ceramic	Stoneware	Glazed	1	1
	Game piece?	Marble?	Ceramic	Stoneware	Salt glaze	2	2
	Game piece?	Marble?	Ceramic	Stoneware	Unadorned	8	8
Total						41	53

Table 17: Summary of provenanced artefacts.

Provenance	Class	Function	MNI
Australia, Melbourne	Glass	Bottle	2
Australia, Sydney	Glass	Bottle	1
Total Australia			*3*
England	Ceramic	Bowl	1
England	Ceramic	Cup	18
England	Ceramic	Dish	5
England	Ceramic	Dish lid	1
England	Ceramic	Jug	4
England	Ceramic	Plate	27
England	Ceramic	Platter	3
England	Ceramic	Pot lid	1
England	Ceramic	Saucer	12
England	Ceramic	Tool	1
England	Ceramic	Tureen	2
England	Ceramic	Tureen lid	1
England	Ceramic	Vessel	14
England, Ashby-De-La-Zouch	Ceramic	Dish	1
England, Burslem	Ceramic	Plate	2
England, London	Ceramic	Bottle	1
England, London	Ceramic	Smoking	1
England, London	Glass	Bottle	2
England, Staffordshire	Ceramic	Bowl	1
England, Staffordshire	Ceramic	Cup	2
England, Staffordshire	Ceramic	Jar	1
England, Staffordshire	Ceramic	Plate	1
England, Staffordshire	Ceramic	Saucer	1
England, Stoke-on-Trent	Ceramic	Platter	1
England, Stoke-on-Trent	Ceramic	Tool	1
England, Stoke-on-Trent	Ceramic	Tureen stand	1
England, Stoke-on-Trent	Ceramic	Vessel	1
England, Tunstall	Ceramic	Plate	1
Total England			*108*
Scotland, Glasgow	Ceramic	Smoking	2
Total Scotland			*2*
Total provenanced			*113*

implements, popular throughout the 19th century (Davies 2005:64). They were commonly associated with children's education (Iacono 1999:78; Ellis 2001), but may also have been used by adults for other purposes such as shopping lists (Davies 2005:63).

Agricultural/Pastoral

The only artefact in the agricultural/pastoral category was 75 percent of a metal file.

PROVENANCE

Only 6 percent of the assemblage could be positively provenanced by makers' marks, with a further 26 percent provenanced by association of a type or decorative technique with a particular country. As **Table 17** shows, the significant majority of provenanced artefacts recovered from the site were made in England, with only small numbers made in Australia and Scotland.

The assemblage recovered from the lower cesspit deposit at 300 Queen Street provides information about the items purchased, used and discarded by the Smith family and possibly their servants. This information will be critically examined in the next chapter in conjunction with the personal histories of the family and the spatial layout of the house presented in earlier chapters.

Life at 300 Queen Street

There was a significant diversity of goods available in Melbourne in the period that the Smiths lived at Queen Street: enough to enable consumer choice and for acquisition to signify cultural capital in the archaeological record. As a precursor to discussing cultural capital, this chapter will examine the interrelationship between the goods chosen by the Smith family, the space they inhabited and life at 300 Queen Street using both the archaeological and historical record.

FAMILY ROLES

Perhaps the most significant artefact relating to the Smith family is the home in which they lived, the manor at 300 Queen Street. The home represented their family ties, security and aspirations. It was the location of private family time, recreation and rest for the couple and their children. Equally their new home in the genteel farming district of Flemington and their seaside retreat at Frankston represent their next step in building a life for their family.

Family bonds outside of the nuclear family were also clearly important to the Smiths. John Thomas Smith's sister Jane lived with the family at 300 Queen Street (*The Argus*, 2 May 1856:5). Smith was also involved with the hotel operations of his father-in-law and brother-in-law after his marriage to Ellen (PROV, VPRS 7/P0, Department of the Treasurer Inward Correspondence (Bound), Index to inward correspondence regarding publicans 1838–1855). The home at Queen Street was located near to these businesses and it is easy to imagine family gatherings there.

As the discussion in this chapter continues, it will become apparent that the home reflects common 19th-century values around family, marriage and childhood. The husband provided for the household and was in command, while the wife and children served and obeyed: notions tightly tied with Christian beliefs (see Davidoff and Hall 2002:108). In this period, life for a middle-class nuclear family was heavily influenced by a gender divide. Historians and historical archaeologists alike have observed the male/public and female/private spheres for middle-class people in the Western world of the 19th century (Saunders and Evans 1992:99; Russell 1994b; Wall 1994; Davidoff and Hall 2002:xvi; Spencer-Wood 2013; Young 2003:18). While this concept influenced daily life, there was inevitable overlap between the spheres with men having a private role as husbands and fathers, and women operating publicly to establish social networks. Saunders and Evans (1992:99) rightly argue that masculine power dominated both spheres, but female support enabled the success and power of middle-class men (Davidoff and Hall 2002:13).

Separate spheres for men and women were also often played out within the middle-class home of the 19th century in the form of gender-specific spaces, most commonly a sitting room for the women and a library or office for the man of the house. The sitting room was explicitly for the purpose of female leisure: sewing, needlework, painting, sketching, flower arranging and music (Bushman 1993:256). In the 19th century, middle-class wives and daughters were involved in domestic duties within the home and often worked alongside the servants (Hourani 1990:74; Russell 1994b:154). When involved in such duties, Mrs Smith and her daughters would also have been relegated to the service areas at the back of the house. This hints at the comparatively lower status of the women of the house than the men (Hourani 1990:74; Yentsch 1991:207). In contrast a library or study was a private, masculine domain (Young 2003:185). Traditionally the library, dedicated to the work and intellectual pursuits of the man of the house, had a strongly masculine character with furnishings that were darker in colour creating a masculine aesthetic (Lane and Serle 1990:134). It is possible that both were present on the ground floor of 300 Queen Street.

Ten of the Smiths' children lived at 300 Queen Street at various stages of infancy, childhood and young adulthood. Much of daily life at the manor would have been centred on the needs of the children. In this period childhood was valued as a precious phase of life and children were increasingly treated as individuals (Davidoff and Hall 2002:343). The act of parenting can be seen in the house itself (as a safe environment), the provision of meals, toys, games and family time.

The Smith children probably shared a number of the upstairs bedrooms at 300 Queen Street. Hourani's (1990:76) archaeological study of Australian middle-class homes of four to 15 rooms indicates that, generally, children's bedrooms were much smaller than the master bedroom. When sharing bedrooms, boys and girls were separated, and ideally also older children from younger children (Flanders 2003:xxv). While it was common in England to have a nursery for the use of children (Davidoff and Hall 2002:375), this was not common in Australia (Hourani 1990; Kociumbas 1997:94, 114). At Queen Street, excluding the master bedroom, there were two smaller bedrooms and one larger room on the first floor. It is possible that all three were children's bedrooms or the larger one may have served as a nursery. A small chamber pot, likely a child's, was made from undecorated whiteware and, in contrast to the elegantly decorated adult chamber pots (**Figure 40**), hints at a certain practicality in providing for the children.

Manufactured toys purchased for children suggest a certain investment in children and reflect 19th-century attitudes to childhood as a special phase of life where children were free to play (Karskens 2001:179). Four toy marbles recovered from Queen Street were simply decorated. Of course, children are more likely to go to greater effort to retrieve more valuable and highly decorated marbles making them less likely to be found in the archaeological record (Wilkie 2000:102). A further 15 marbles were undecorated with 12 of these possibly being pie baking weights (to weight the base while blind baking). Interestingly, two of the supposed pie baking weights were recovered housed in a bark case. It is possible that a child made this toy out of handy items: a tobacco case and baking weights. A metal toy cannon with a barrel and two wheels may have been a prized possession, accidentally lost or merely outgrown.

Toys could also play an important role, particularly for girls, in teaching manners and domestic duties (Praetzellis and Praetzellis 1992:92). A fluted whiteware plate from a doll's tea set would have served to educate the Smith girls about the etiquette of paying calls and receiving visitors (Fitts 1999:54). When purchased by adults they can be seen as purposeful attempts to enforce and encourage certain behaviour (Wilkie 2000:101).

A porcelain doll's head with hand-painted black hair, pink cheeks and red mouth, and a ceramic figurine with reversible happy and sad faces were found at Queen Street. Most 19th-century dolls depicted adults, and their aim was to enforce female identity as well as educating girls regarding fashion and etiquette (Wilkie 2000:102).

The six slate pencils recovered from the cesspit may have played a role in the education of the children. Slate pencils and writing slates were cheap and durable writing implements often used in teaching (Iacono 1999:78; Ellis 2001; Davies 2005:64) and again this is suggestive of investment in children (Yamin 2002:118). There is no record of the education of the girls, whether at a school or by a governess. The education they did receive probably focused on their moral character and manners rather than intellectual pursuits (Russell 1994b:145–146). The lives of the Smiths' four daughters while still at home would have been closely intertwined with

each other and their mother. A number of feminine pursuits would have been undertaken in a social setting including handiwork, shopping and paying calls (Hayes 2014:13). Details of the Smith boys' early education were not found in the historical record; however, it is clear that formal education was a high priority with their eldest son going on to become a barrister and the youngest a medical practitioner (BDM VIC 9638d/1901; De Serville 1991:438; BDM QLD B35080d/1921 p.1522).

It is unclear how important religion was to the daily life of the Smith family and no religious artefacts were recovered from the cesspit. John Thomas Smith belonged to the Church of England, but Ellen was from an Irish Catholic background even though inter-marriage between the faiths was frowned upon at the time. It appears that the Smith children were raised Church of England: a number of the children's marriages and deaths were presided over in the Church of England (BDM VIC 1309m/1861, 2609m/1875, 3790m/1879, 7986d/1886, 10455d/1895).

SERVANTS

Neither the historical records nor the archaeological evidence at 300 Queen Street reveal much regarding the servants employed at the manor house. However, a household of this size and in this period would have, no doubt, been run to a large extent by servants. An article in the *Geelong Advertiser* (17 October 1848:1) mentions that 'Mr Smith's servants resided in the theatre' a short 280m walk from the manor. Some servants, such as a housekeeper or nanny, may have lived at 300 Queen Street. The housekeeper sometimes had a bedroom on the same level as the family but this room was significantly smaller. Room F6 at 300 Queen Street looks very much like a housekeeper's bedroom (**Figure 16**).

The comfort of 300 Queen Street for the Smith family was unlikely to have been echoed for the servants who worked there. The kitchen and scullery, where the servants were predominantly based, was divided from the rest of the house (Flanders 2003:xxv). The service areas were often cramped and simply decorated reinforcing the low status of the servants within the household (Hourani 1990:74).

Part of this relegation and division was to control interaction with family (Russell 1994b:169, 172). Careful negotiation dictated when certain tasks, such as cleaning, making beds, emptying chamber pots, bringing in firewood, lighting fires, lighting lamps etc., would take place (Russell 1993:30; Griffin 2004:50).

The uglier side of the servants' work (cooking, laundry, cleaning etc.) was kept hidden from visitors (Bushman 1993:262). However, the presence of servants in front of visitors also functioned as a display of wealth and status. Servants were expected to answer the door and wait on guests: a process that was carefully controlled through servants' bells (Hayes 2008:290–292, 2014:41, 69).

The carefully constructed hierarchy of servants would have also influenced their experience at 300 Queen Street. A butler or housekeeper held a respected position within the household while general maids would never have been seen by visitors and, for that matter, the family. Middle-class women had to negotiate class boundaries with their servants and uphold important social distinctions. The threat of the influence of the lowly morals of the working class, especially on children, was a serious concern at the time and servants were expected to maintain standards of decorum (Davidoff and Hall 2002:395).

DINING

Ordinary events of daily life can be indicators of wealth and social position. Wealth enabled display and leisure, while the cultural capital of various social positions subtly influenced decisions around consumption and behaviour. One of the key areas where this played out, and frequently the one that is most archaeologically visible, is that of dining.

Eating was about so much more than sustenance in the 19th century: wealth, ceremony, display, ritual, comportment and manners all came in to play (Fitts 1999; Young 2003:182; Russell 2010:216). How meals were executed was an important indicator of position in society. Contrast, for example, a simple meal served in bowls and eaten with spoons to a multi-course meal served at the table out of elaborately decorated tableware. Wealth and knowledge about etiquette were key elements in executing a dining experience in the genteel manner.

Meals at 300 Queen Street would have followed the prescribed expectations for middle-class dining in this period (see, for example, Beeton 1861). Breakfasts, lunches and dinners had varying levels of formality requiring different tableware. Breakfasts and lunches were less formal, but nevertheless required purpose-specific sets of tableware. Breakfast was served early and usually included one hot meat dish and toast with tea (Flanders 2003:225). Men would have lunch at work, while women and children would have a light cooked lunch at home often utilising leftovers (Flanders 2003:225; Mitchell 2009:126). There were three major types of dinners: weeknight dinners, Sunday dinners and dinner parties (Mitchell 2009:126). On week nights, adult members of the family generally dined alone in the dining room, children in the nursery, and servants in the kitchen. Children and servants generally received simple meat and potato meals (Flanders 2003:225), with the adult family members receiving more substantial and varied fare.

Matching sets of ceramics and purpose-specific vessels played an important role in presenting and serving each type of meal in the prescribed manner.

Of the nine matching tableware sets recovered from the 300 Queen Street cesspit (tea sets will be discussed later), five were actual matches and four were complementary matches (see Chapter 5). A notable majority, 64 percent, of the tableware was part of a set. Vessels from nine sets made their way into the cesspit over the 11-year period that the Smiths were at Queen Street and there may have been many more sets not discarded. From the Viewbank tip, 62 percent of the tableware vessels were from 11 actual matching sets and three complementary sets. The Viewbank tip, though not completely excavated, was used over a much longer period of time: approximately 30 years (Hayes 2014:23, 29).

Sets were clearly important at 300 Queen Street, with different sets for different meals, including probably for the children and servants. The largest, most expensive and most elaborate sets would have been reserved for Sunday meals and the presence of guests. The two most expensively decorated sets were the flow, hand-painted and gilt Chinoise pattern set and the transfer-printed and hand-painted Chinese flowers pattern set. Both sets included plates and serving vessels and were most likely used for formal dinners. Other expensive, large sets in timeless designs may have been kept and handed down to the next generation (Hayes 2014:66). The flow transfer-printed and gilt 'Dagger Border' plates may have been for the more formal Sunday dinners. The 'Alpine' pattern set could have been a week night dinner set for the adult family members; it included plates, a tureen and tea service vessels (see discussion below). The 'Asiatic Pheasants' set may have been for everyday dinners or lunches. These sets still maintained a level of formality with a number of purpose-specific vessels. If representing complete sets, it is possible that the gilded and sprigged sets, which comprised both food and tea service vessels, were used for breakfasts. The flow transfer and hand-painted egg cups also may have been part of a formal breakfast set. Casey (2005:104) argues that simply decorated banded, moulded or plain vessels in tea and tableware forms were multipurpose sets not designated to lunch or dinner. The simple sets at Queen Street, such as the 'Willow' and complementary common gilt and sprigged sets may have been such multi-purpose sets or used by the servants and children.

Formal dinner services required a range of vessel forms and purpose-specific vessels (Shackel 1993:30–42; Fitts 1999:54). A standard dinner service could include 80 to 140 vessels with a range of plate sizes, sauce tureens, soup tureens, platters, serving dishes, butter dishes, pitchers and gravy boats (Fitts 1999:182; Young 2003). In the archaeological record, such variety in vessel forms are associated with more elaborate table etiquette (Yentsch 1991:221). Plates were the most common tableware vessel form at 300 Queen Street, but purpose-specific vessels including egg cups, dishes, platters and tureens were also present.

Tea service also required matching sets and purpose-specific vessels. In the Queen Street assemblage, 64 percent of the teaware vessels were part of a set. As with tableware, a number of tea sets were required to cater for different types of teas: when guests called, between meals and for servants (Hayes 2014:66). The 'Alpine' pattern set comprised the most tea service vessels and also included food service vessels: twiffler plates (smaller than a dinner plate but larger than a side plate) and a tureen. This set may have been for breakfast or afternoon tea. The transfer-printed 'Vignette' and flow transfer Chinese scene tea sets were relatively less expensive than the 'Alpine' and may have been used for tea between meals. The complementary common gilt and sprigged sets also had tableware vessels and may have been multi-purpose or for use by the servants (see Hayes 2014:66).

No teapots or sugar bowls were recovered by the excavation. It is possible that this was because a silver tea service was used. As silver has an intrinsic value in spite of changing fashions it is likely that any silverware would have been retained or handed down to one of the children (Hayes 2014:66).

The nature and type of decoration on the 300 Queen Street tablewares differs to other Victorian domestic archaeological assemblages of this era in that there was a much higher instance (40 percent of the total) of multiple decorations and multi-coloured tablewares. Archaeological evidence suggests that Australians preferred colourful tableware, transfer-printed, flow transfer etc., in accordance with British and British colonial tastes (Lawrence 2003:25, 26; Brooks 2010). Single colour transfer-printed patterns frequently dominate working-class assemblages in both Victoria (Lawrence 2000:131–132; Williamson 2006:330; Prossor et al. 2012:820) and elsewhere in Australia (Karskens 1999:94–95; Crook et al. 2005:151). At middle-class Viewbank homestead 27.4 percent of the tableware had multiple decorations and 23 percent was undecorated or plain moulded (Hayes 2014:29). When I broke down the multiple decoration category into two types: 1) those combining decorative techniques such as transfer-printing, hand-painting and gilt into a colourfully decorated ceramic, and 2) those with a simple decoration such as transfer-print or gilt combined with moulding; an interesting pattern emerged. At Viewbank, 15.3 percent of the tableware in the multiple decorations category were moulded and gilded, or moulded and transfer-printed leaving only 12.1 percent of the tableware combining decorative techniques into a colourfully decorated ceramic. In the Queen Street assemblage, the number of colourfully decorated, multiple technique ceramics was 38.2 percent. This creates the impression that the tableware at 300 Queen Street was more grandiose and showy than that found not only at working-class sites, but also at the 'established middle-class' Viewbank homestead. Consumer choice with regard to tableware decoration preferences were determined by wealth, class and what message the owners tried to be express.

In contrast to the tableware, the teaware at 300 Queen Street was somewhat more demure. Single colour decorations dominated the teawares with 48 percent being flow transfer prints and 21 percent being transfer prints, and there was a strong preference for blue above other colours. This is a very different pattern to Viewbank homestead where 10.8 percent of the teawares were flow and 10.8 percent were transfer-printed. Gilded teawares dominated at Viewbank with 23.1 percent followed by multiple decorations with 19.2 percent. However, only 6.9 percent of the multiple decoration teawares combined colourful techniques rather than simply moulding as the second technique (Hayes 2014:33–34). It is possible that this difference represents different uses of the teawares at 300 Queen Street as compared to Viewbank. As part of the 'established middle class', receiving calls would have been very important for the Martins at Viewbank. This may not have been the case at 300 Queen Street and, as such, elaborately decorated teawares may not have been required. The meaning of the differences between the tableware and teaware at Viewbank and Queen Street will be examined in more detail in the next chapter.

It would appear that the Smiths made some effort to keep up with fashions in their purchasing of ceramics, particularly for the tableware. While the dating of the ceramics from 300 Queen Street does little to indicate how frequently tableware and teaware were updated, the fact that 45.5 percent of the vessels were more than 75 percent complete might suggest that they were discarded while serviceable purely because they were out of fashion.

Flaws were noted on all of the tableware and teaware vessels with similar levels of severity between the two (see Chapter 5). It is possible that the Smiths were able to purchase more elaborately decorated sets of ceramics by choosing flawed seconds (see Crook 2011:591). While a certain number of flaws were an inevitable part of 19th-century ceramic manufacturing techniques (Crook 2011:584), a small number of the ceramics at 300 Queen Street were significantly flawed. Evidence from Crook's (2008:254) research suggests that in Sydney consumers had access to the same range of goods as people in London and this is also likely to be the case for Melbourne. Purchasing significantly flawed ceramics was therefore likely to have been a purposeful consumer strategy for the Smiths (Hayes 2017:8).

Glass vessels also served an important role in serving condiments, sides and desserts. A heavy shallow glass dish found in the Queen Street cesspit was possibly a salt cellar and two other glass vessels, though fragmentary and of unidentified form, may have been on the table at meal times. Condiments were an important part of improving and brightening dull meals, and a number of condiment storage containers were recovered from the cesspit at 300 Queen Street: three bung jars for olives, gherkins, onions or capers (Lawrence 2006:79), a probable jam jar, a Staffordshire mustard jar, glass pickle bottles and a fluted salad oil/vinegar bottle. Such condiments would have been decanted into decorative vessels for service at the table as part of formal dining. However, for everyday meals for the servants and children the mustard, pickle and oil bottles were likely to have been considered sufficiently decorative to be placed on the table. Further, two wooden cutlery handles, probably from knives, may have been utilitarian and used by the servants when dining or in the preparation of food.

The tableware recovered from the 300 Queen Street cesspit represents only what the Smiths discarded in a limited time period. It is likely that they owned, kept or discarded elsewhere even more sets and vessels. Even so, the number and nature of the tableware recovered indicates the Smiths were catering for a variety of levels of formality in meals for the different occupants of the house and for visitors.

DRINKING AND SMOKING

Given John Thomas Smith's involvement in the operation of hotels, it is easy to imagine that drinking alcohol was an enjoyable aspect of life at 300 Queen Street. Stemmed drinking glasses were used for wine, champagne, claret and cordial while tumblers were used for ale, whiskey, soda water, lemonade and iced tea (Jones 2000:224–225). Sixteen tumblers, five wine glasses, three port/sherry glasses and two possible champagne glasses were recovered from the cesspit. This selection of glassware certainly supports the notion that alcohol was consumed at Queen Street.

A variety of both pressed and cut decoration on the glasses and the range of forms suggest that different glass sets were used for different purposes in a similar manner to the ceramic tableware. Five identical pressed Gothic arch tumblers formed a set and when used at the table would have complemented the matching ceramic tableware. The cut glass tumblers, wine glasses, champagne glasses and port/sherry glasses were relatively more refined and expensive and may have originally been in sets reserved for formal dining (Jones 2000:174).

As noted in Chapter 5, the form of a beverage bottle may not in fact reflect the contents that were purchased in the bottle. Bottles, both marked and unmarked, were extensively reused in the 19th century with beverage manufacturers purchasing bottles from second-hand bottle dealers (Busch 1991; Woff 2014; Ellis and Woff 2017). Bottles were washed and reused many times and for different liquids (Carney 1998; Woff 2014). Australian beverage manufacturers were largely refilling imported bottles, and the majority of bottles found in the Queen Street cesspit were most likely to have been imported and possibly refilled with a different beverage from what the vessel form would imply.

At 300 Queen Street, 40 percent of the beverage storage bottles were of an ubiquitous beer/wine form which were used for any number of beverages (Busch 1991:113–116). Champagne, wine and gin bottles were also recovered from the cesspit and may have been slightly more likely to contain the beverage suggested by the form when purchased than the beer/wine form. Nine torpedo-shaped aerated water bottles were designed specifically to retain the aeration and, given they do not sit flat on their bases, are unlikely to have been refilled with any other beverage. A further two stoneware bottle finishes were of the style used to house ginger beer and a large cream stoneware bottle may have originally contained spirits. Two glass decanter stoppers suggest that care was taken to decant spirits or sherry into decorative containers, and four jugs may have been used to serve beverages (but note that jugs were also used as vases in this period).

Wine was locally produced and readily available from the very early years of the Port Phillip district with numerous vineyards in operation in Melbourne, Geelong and the Yarra Valley (Beeston 1994:38, 49). Labour shortages during the gold rushes meant that the wine industry faltered, but many returned to winemaking in the 1860s as the rushes waned (Beeston 1994:47–48; Dunstan 1994:34). In addition to vineyards, by the mid-1840s there were six breweries operating in Melbourne, but the quality remained poor. In the early 1860s there were 20 breweries in Melbourne, and by 1874 there were 31 (Deutsher 1999:87). During the 1860s, there were also 80 breweries operating in 34 country towns in Victoria (Deutsher 1999:88). In addition, there were 20 manufacturers of ginger beer, cordial and aerated water operating in Melbourne by 1863 (Davies 2006:348). A wide range of locally produced beverages was available and the archaeological evidence, while not conclusive, suggests that both alcoholic and non-alcoholic beverages were enjoyed at 300 Queen Street.

With regard to smoking, the presence of a minimum number of 18 clay pipes in the 300 Queen Street cesspit is interesting. Clay pipes in the archaeological record generally have a working-class association, with briar pipes, cigarettes and snuff associated with the middle and upper classes (Walker 1984:4; Gojak and Stuart 1999:40; McCarthy 2001:150). The presence of such a large number suggests to me that it may in fact be the Smiths who were smoking clay pipes rather than the servants. Note that at Viewbank homestead only four clay pipes were recovered from a tip which was used over a much longer period than the cesspit at Queen Street (Hayes 2014:63). Further, the majority of the servants employed at Queen Street lived elsewhere so it is less likely that their pipes would be discarded at the manor. There is reference to John Thomas Smith smoking a cutty shape pipe (Eastwood 1976:150), but both clay and more fancy briar types were made in this shape. It is possible, therefore, that John Thomas and/or Ellen Smith were keeping to their working-class roots and smoking clay pipes at home.

SOCIAL EVENTS

In his role as Mayor, it would have been necessary for John Thomas Smith to host dinners and events for influential members of Melbourne society. A large number of sets and quality tableware in an archaeological assemblage suggest that the tools required for entertaining were available (Yamin 1998:82). At 300 Queen Street the presence of formal and highly decorated ceramic sets would have enabled the Smiths to host suitably sophisticated dinner parties. Governor Sir Henry Barkly dined at 300 Queen Street (De Serville 1991) and other official dinners would have been hosted there.

The manor at Queen Street had both a dining and drawing room on the ground floor (see Chapter 4). The two rooms comprised the public space of the house, with the drawing room an English adaptation specifically designed for social interaction (Davidoff and Hall 2002:377). Both rooms were formal and presented the home to guests. The dining and drawing rooms would have been the main location for parties. In addition, in this period, furniture was often rearranged in order to take advantage of more rooms and space (Russell 1994b:74; Young 2003:74–75).

Paying and receiving calls played a vital role in the maintenance of social networks in Melbourne, signifying social acceptance and importance. Calls were made out of courtesy to new acquaintances or as a thank you for hospitality, as congratulations upon a birth or marriage, or condolence on the death of a family member (Russell 1994b:50–51). The custom was transplanted from England and was prevalent in the colonies. Tea would be served, and calls would last from 15 to 30 minutes (Mitchell 2009:151). Women would often take embroidery or fancy work with them when calling on the women of other households (Beaudry 2006:106). While predominantly the domain of women, boys and men would also occasionally attend calls (Russell 1994b:51).

In Melbourne society, calls served not only to establish social networks but also to exclude those not deemed to be sufficiently genteel and of good character (Russell 1994b:50). The tea service artefacts recovered from the cesspit at 300 Queen Street were less elaborate than the dinner wares, for which I see three possible interpretations. First,

that the Smiths were excluded from the circle of calls undertaken by the 'established middle class'; second, that it was not as important to them as hosting dinners; and third, that they may have had their own network of friends who paid calls but were less concerned with display in this area. The nuanced way in which families such as the Smiths were both excluded and included in social interactions will be discussed in more detail in the next chapter.

LEISURE

Leisure for the middle class in the 19th century was about family time, relaxation, self-improvement and building social networks. Games were likely to be an important part of shared family evenings, but no game related items were recovered from the 300 Queen Street cesspit. Other evening pastimes included reading (often aloud) (Russell 1994b:157), playing music and sewing. The chosen leisure activities served the purpose of educating children in vital skills such as literacy but also comportment and behaviour. Leisured evenings were defined by the refined lifestyle of the middle class and values around domesticity. However, I imagine that such evenings for the Smiths and other 'aspirational middle class' Melbournians had a somewhat less genteel ilk than those customary at the homes of the 'established middle class'.

For women, there was a strong emphasis on productive leisure and this frequently comprised sewing, needlework, painting and flower arranging (Russell 1994b:97). Embroidery and decorative needlework were symbols of feminine, leisured lifestyle and can be uncovered archaeologically (Lydon 1993b:129–130). Social expectations in the 19th century demanded that daughters, regardless of class, were taught to sew by their mothers, and not doing so could bring disapproval (Parker 1984:9; Beaudry 2006:105).

Only four sewing related artefacts were recovered from the cesspit at 300 Queen Street: a lace-making bobbin, thimble, thread on a leather spool, and a possible thread reel holder made of bone. While I am tempted to interpret the small sewing assemblage as meaning that the Smith women were not interested in this highly genteel and demure pursuit, it is also possible that the absence of sewing items merely reflects the fact that they were not discarded in the cesspit and may have been lost or discarded elsewhere.

The thimble, spool and possible thread reel holder may have been used at 300 Street for utilitarian needlework including sewing, mending, and remaking garments, sheets and linens (Beaudry 2006:5). Servants were often employed in practical needlework, but depending on means, middle-class women would also perform mending and making dresses or other large items of clothing (Flanders 2003:223, 265; Mitchell 2009:230).

The lace bobbin recovered from the cesspit

indicates that the luxury item, lace, was being made by hand at 300 Queen Street. Although machine-made lace was available in the second half of the 19th century (Sykes 1988:3–4), lace-making bobbins are frequently recovered from archaeological sites from this period suggesting that handmade lace was still popular. While some lace was made by genteel ladies as a delicate art, lace-making was also an important cottage industry in Britain and its colonies well into the 19th century (Beaudry 2006:151–152). Lace-making may have been a leisure activity for Ellen Smith and her daughters, or it is possible that a servant was employed in this task.

Leisure outside the home was an important part of building social networks. The Queen's Theatre was a short walk from the Smiths' house; their servants lived there and the Smiths were probably regular audience members. In the second half of the 19th century in Australia, there was much debate and effort to regulate theatres and make them well-ordered spaces. Ultimately, however, they were used by many classes in their own ways (Russell 2010:294). The first years of the Queen's Theatre catered for both tastes but the emphasis gradually shifted to more respectable concerts, classical music performances by highly regarded musicians and charity fundraisers (see Chapter 3). The Smith family would have doubtless attended the theatre, but the tone and type of performances they attended is unknown.

SHOPPING

Shopping served a number of purposes for Melbournians at this time: to acquire goods, as a leisure activity and for socialising. Living in the centre of Melbourne gave the Smiths access to a variety of shopping opportunities, and Crook's (2008:254) research has shown that the range of goods available in Australian cities rivalled that in London. The archaeological record rarely reveals much with regard to shopping. In some instances, shop names on objects such as buttons or combs can indicate where goods were purchased but no shop names were identified on artefacts in the 300 Queen Street assemblage. However, historical accounts give some insight into how the Smiths would have shopped.

Fashionable inner-city shops, arcades and department stores demanded a certain level of wealth from the customers and therefore predominantly catered to the middle class (Kingston 1994:26; Crook 2000:19–20). The hustle and bustle of open-air markets provided for the working class and goods there were more affordable (Crook 2000:17). Crook (2000:24) has argued that in working-class assemblages a mix of luxury and poor quality items might be the result of the influence of affordability and availability of second-hand goods in market bazaars, with a small number of valuable items the result of theft, gambling or heirlooms being handed down. Adding to this, in my work on Viewbank I argued that cohesion in an assemblage with many expensive goods, matching sets and consistent quality items suggest shopping in stores and arcades (Hayes 2014:58). The large number of matching sets recovered from the Queen Street cesspit suggest that the Smiths were able to purchase complete sets at one time possibly from shops, but the large number of flawed vessels noted in the assemblage makes it clear that they also accessed the seconds market for cheaper alternatives (Hayes 2017).

When the Smiths moved to Queen Street, there were no shopping arcades or department stores in Melbourne, but increasing numbers of fashionable shops opened as the years went by and Melbourne became more established. Draper and haberdasher Buckley and Nunn opened in 1852, and later expanded into a department store (Priestley 1984:135). The first arcade in Melbourne was the Queen's arcade opened in 1853, with a number of others following. Arcades incorporated a range of elegant shops protected from the elements and have been an enduring element of Melbourne shopping. By the 1860s, just when the Smiths were leaving Queen Street, window displays of tempting goods lured pedestrians from the sidewalks into the shops (Brown-May 1998:52) and around the world many general stores and draperies were developing into department stores (Kingston 1994:27–28).

Collins Street was Melbourne's premier shopping street by mid-century, and traders carried a wide range of imported goods in fashionable shops, including household wares, furniture, clothing and jewellery (Priestley 1984:23–26). Being seen on Collins Street, and spending appropriate amounts of money on fashionable goods, was an important opportunity for socialising for genteel Melbourne society. However, drawing on historical records Russell (2010:276–277) reveals that there were varying opinions of Collins Street in the 1860s. Clara Aspinall, a visitor to Melbourne, regarded Collins Street as a genteel and pleasant place to be, while Coroner Curtis Candler was concerned by the mix of social levels shopping there and the difficulty in discerning the ranks of shoppers (Aspinall 1862:8; Russell 2010:276–277).

The Smiths were probably among this mix of people shopping at Collins Street. No record exists of the shops they frequented; however, a controversial episode in 1856 involved the 'removal', allegedly with permission, by Ellen and Jane (John Thomas Smith's sister) of quality fabrics and goods from the shop of a deceased relative on Collins Street (more on this in the next chapter). They took silk, satin and 14 yards of merino fabric, silk umbrellas, silk and satin dresses, socks, shirts, handkerchiefs, neck handkerchiefs and hosiery (*The Argus*, 2 May 1856:5). The selection of goods is suggestive of the access to finery in Melbourne at the time.

Testimony during the court proceeding that followed estimated the value of the shop stock at £4000 to £5000 (*The Argus*, 2 May 1856:5) at a time when a domestic servant earnt around £12 to £28 per year (Higman 2002:170). The Smith women's desire for luxury items and familiarity with Collins Street are apparent in this tale, and so too is the underhanded nature in which the women set about obtaining the goods. They recognised and valued quality, and liked the idea of getting something for nothing.

The Smiths may have purchased some of their goods through mail order. It was possible to order household goods and personal items directly from London stores to avoid the physical environment of shopping and to get the most up-to-date items (Kingston 1994:25). Trade catalogues sold anything from toothbrushes to furniture, and postal orders were a popular way to purchase goods in 19th-century Australia (see Crook 2005).

At the time the Smiths lived at 300 Queen Street, most Melbournians shopped for their food at open-air markets in the CBD (Cannon 1975:33). The Western Market, located at the corner of Collins Street and Williams Street, was less than one kilometre from the Smiths' residence. The hustle and bustle of markets were generally avoided by the middle class and the Smiths probably sent their servants to shop on their behalf.

Access to goods in the 19th century was increasingly globalised, facilitated by industrialised mass production and new technologies for transporting goods. Recent studies (Crook 2008, 2011; Rodriguez and Brooks 2012) show how globalised domestic purchasing was becoming at this time. Global trade networks reflect not only economic networks but also social networks, and the provenance of artefacts in archaeological assemblages can be used to interpret the meanings behind consumer choices (Adams 1991).

Discussion of the origin of artefacts from the Smiths' residence is limited to objects with makers' marks, or where possible other features, that positively identify their place of manufacture. Although this may not reveal all the sources of goods in the assemblage, it does indicate the general patterns of access to trade networks. Of the artefacts recovered from the cesspit, 30 percent could be associated with a country of manufacture.

Of the small percentage of goods that had a place of provenance, 96 percent were from England with an additional 1 percent from Scotland, and 3 percent from Australia (**Table 17**). The dominance of English goods was in part due to their widespread availability in the colony, but a desire for them because of familiarity or cultural preference likely drove consumer choice (Hayes 2014:57). The British goods in the Queen Street assemblage were predominantly ceramics but glass bottles and clay pipes were also present. Trading power and dominance were not the only factors influencing their presence; there was a genuine demand for British goods which expressed middle class values, behaviours and beliefs (Young 2003:7–8). The Scottish goods were two clay pipes and a beer/wine bottle, while the Australian goods were an aerated water bottle and a beer/wine bottle.

This preference for English goods is one side of the coin: on the other, the absence of goods from other exporting countries, such as Chinese storage vessels, Chinese or Japanese ceramics, French alcohol or German toys is also noteworthy. At Viewbank there were a number of such items in the assemblage (Hayes 2014:57) and this might suggest that a preference for exotic and luxury items or the ability to purchase them was the domain of the upper levels of society. This was something that the Smiths lacked either the purchasing power for or the interest in.

A significant proportion of the food and drink purchased by the Smiths was likely produced in Australia, aside from alcohol and preserved goods which could be imported. Market gardens, farms, orchards and dairies were established around Melbourne from the earliest years and provided for the needs of residents (Gaynor 2005:277–278). As noted above, wine, beer and non-alcoholic beverages were all produced in Victoria. However, most of this produce would not leave a trace of origin in the archaeological record. Beverages were rarely sold in a container that identified the contents as being made in Australia, with most being sold in imported and reused bottles (Woff 2014). While there was some early demand for Australian made glass bottles and production in Sydney from the 1860s, it was not until 1872 that the first successful glass manufacturer commenced operations in Melbourne (Vader 1975:14; Graham 1981:15–17; Hayes 2014:52–53). Stoneware bottles were produced in Sydney from the early 19th century and Melbourne from the 1850s (Ford 1995:176–293). Only rarely did such bottles carry a makers' mark that identified them as being Australian made. While the Smiths probably purchased Australian goods and possibly goods from other countries, the marked artefacts in the assemblage suggest a strong preference for English goods.

PERSONAL APPEARANCE

Melbournians in the 19th century were very concerned with fashion, and while it was an important mechanism in defining status it was not always easy to interpret a person's position based on dress. Decent people could dress gaudily while lower ranked people could dress respectably (Russell 2010:276–277). Paris and London fashions were closely observed in Melbourne in this era and clothes were either imported from Europe, or made locally (Maynard 1994:85).

For men, attire conveyed their status and power. Fashion for middle-class men was as important and essentially the same as in Europe, but with greater variety noted in the colony (Maynard 1994:82–83). A handful of items recovered from the cesspit hint at Smith's concern with his appearance, or possibly that of his teenage sons. Smith is depicted in **Figure 41** holding an umbrella: a walking stick or umbrella handle was found in the cesspit. Walking sticks were an elegant, rather than necessary, accessory for men. Macassar hair oil and a wooden hairbrush found may also have been used by the Smith men. The four Prosser buttons found in the cesspit may have been from undergarments or shirts worn by Smith or his sons (or, equally, women's or children's clothing) and the bone and wood buttons may have been from a coat, jacket or trousers (Birmingham 1992:105; Lindbergh 1999:53–54; Sprague 2002:124).

De Serville (1991:21) noted that the wives of the newly rich 'were preoccupied with dress to the exclusion of serious matters.' Apparently respectable wives and daughters would dress in flashy attire (Russell 2010:277) and such observations seemingly fit with the Smith women. Ellen and sister-in-law Jane had a penchant for fine clothing, choosing high quality silk and satin dresses, gloves and jewellery when they helped themselves to stock in their deceased relative's store (more on this in next chapter) (*The Argus*, 2 May 1856:5).

Figure 42: John Thomas Smith, 1863 (Creator: Samuel Calvert; Source: State Library of Victoria, www.slv.vic.gov.au).

Evidence from the cesspit assemblage suggests that this preoccupation with appearance extended to makeup and perfume. Eight ceramic pots likely contained ointment or cosmetics and two small ceramic dishes may have been cosmetic palettes. A mirror fragment recovered fits with this picture. Three perfume bottles, two in expensive cut glass, show an ability to expend money on a luxury item that enhanced how the women were perceived.

A spectacle lens was recovered from the Queen Street cesspit. While spectacles were a necessity for those with poor vision, they were also popular in the 19th century as a decorative accessory that gave an air of dignity to the wearer (Iacono 1999:72). Women often used long gold chains to hold spectacles, tucked in a pocket (Young 2003:171) and monocles and pincers were popular among men.

The nuances of fashion in 19th-century Melbourne required great effort to ensure that one's appearance remained genteel and not vulgar (Russell 1994b). John Thomas Smith was known for his dapper appearance, but at the same time there was a tone of mockery in the newspapers of the day implying that Smith was getting above himself in his showy approximation of a regal appearance (**Figure 41** and **Figure 42**).

Figure 41: Detail from 'A Group of City Fathers, 1862' showing John Thomas Smith in his white top hat (Publisher: Alfred Martin Ebsworth; Source: State Library of Victoria, www.slv.vic.gov.au).

HEALTH AND HYGIENE

In mid-19th-century Melbourne, residents had access to both prescription and proprietary medicines through doctors and chemists. Six chemists or druggists were already open in Melbourne in 1842, and by 1860 this number had grown to 88 (Knehans 2005:42). The presence of medicine bottles on archaeological sites from this period is common and by no means limited to the wealthy. At 300 Queen Street 25 medicine bottles in a variety of shapes and sizes were recovered from the cesspit and suggest that a variety of medicines were used by the Smiths including small bottles for single dose medicines and a bottle stopper from a dispensary or druggist bottle.

Doctors of this era often treated patients in perilous ways with heavy doses of drugs, bleeding and purging (Davies 2001:63). These treatments often did more harm than good and in the second half of the century there was growing concern over who could call themselves a doctor, with many practitioners having little or no qualifications. In 1862, the *Medical Practitioners Act* was passed to enforce controls on who could practice in Victoria and how (Knehans 2005:42). At the same time, Victorians were keen users of self-dosed proprietary medicines to maintain health and wellbeing, many of which were imported (Davies 2006:352).

It is very difficult to distinguish between prescription and proprietary medicines from bottle shape alone as there was much blurring of the boundaries between prescription and proprietary medicine in the 19th century. Although medical practitioners predominantly treated patients and prescribed medicines, while chemists prepared and dispensed them, there was considerable overlap in these roles (Knehans 2005:41). Chemists would often provide customers with a diagnosis and then recommend the medicines they had prepared (Hagger 1979:167).

It is difficult to discern more details from the archaeological record on the types of medicine contained by the bottles recovered from Queen Street. Bottles dispensed by chemists often used paper labels and bottles were taken back to the store for re-filling – usually with the same, but sometimes a different, medicine (Knehans 2005:45). Paper labels rarely survive in archaeological deposits and medicines purchased in tins, boxes and packets generally decay leaving no trace in the archaeological record (Graham 2005:52). As a result we know that the Smiths were using a variety of medicines but can tell very little about what those medicines were or the ailments they treated.

A growing obsession with cleanliness was taking hold in the 19th century with advisory literature carefully outlining the means and frequency of bathing and personal care. Washing daily either in a bath, or a sponge bath for the face, neck, groin, hands and feet was recommended (Flanders 2003:288–289; Young 2003:97). A basin and ewer in the bedroom on a custom-built washstand allowed for washing in the privacy of the bedroom. Sponge baths, hip baths and shower baths became increasingly popular from the 1830s on, as interest in cleanliness and the health-giving properties of water grew (Young 2003:100–102).

Toilet sets became popular and could include a basin, ewer, soap dish, sponge bowl, toothbrush jar, and slop pail (Young 2003:98), and double toilet sets were available for shared bedrooms. A black transfer-printed soap dish was the only toilet item recovered from the Queen Street cesspit. In addition to toilet sets, chamber pots were an essential part of hygiene in the bedroom. The chamber pot was preferable to a night time walk to the outdoor cesspit. Chamber pots were often housed in a purpose built cupboard, drawer or chair that would conceal the contents (Young 2003:109). A minimum of three chamber pots, and possibly two more, were recovered from the cesspit. The full size chamber pots were either transfer-printed or flow transfer-printed and a small, child-size chamber pot was unadorned.

Toothbrushes are also frequently found on 19th-century domestic sites and Queen Street was no exception: three bone-handled toothbrushes were found in the cesspit. Toothbrushes became increasingly mass-produced and widespread throughout the 19th century (Young 2003:104). The Smiths clearly had the means, knowledge and motivation to invest in their health and hygiene.

The goods chosen by the Smiths and recovered from the cesspit rubbish deposit at 300 Queen Street, along with historical records and evidence from their home, give an insight into the daily life of the family from dining to shopping. Much of the Smiths' lives were played out following the dictates of 19th-century middle-class values; however, there are suggestions in the material culture selected by the Smiths that they were not merely conforming but playing out their own values and employing cultural capital in ways to achieve their goals. How they employed this cultural capital will be the topic of the next chapter.

Cultural Capital and the Road to Success

This chapter turns to the question: what was the role of cultural capital in the Smith family's success at leaving behind the convict stain and their working class roots to become influential and affluent members of Melbourne's middle class? The reconstruction of daily life in the previous chapter will now form the basis of examining the interrelationship of gentility and respectability for the Smiths within the context of the changing nature of Melbourne society. As we will see, cultural capital – uniquely applied to their position and purpose – was an important aspect of the Smiths' road to success and in shaping the newly formed Melbourne society.

SITUATING THE SMITHS

There is no doubt that John Thomas Smith moved up from his parents' convict roots and became very successful (*The Australian News for Home Readers*, 25 January 1864:14; *The Argus*, 31 January 1879:6). In spite of this, he never could shake the shadow of his background and was dogged by scandalous innuendo, but how this influenced his life is unclear. Much of the historical information pertaining to Smith comes from *The Argus*, Melbourne's foremost newspaper at the time, and the editors (including William Kerr, Edward Wilson and Lauchlan Mackinnon) clearly despised Smith. The sense of the man that comes from this source is of a cut-throat, underhanded, self-made man who was not considered acceptable by society in taste, action or behaviour (*The Melbourne Argus*, 23 November 1847:2; *The Argus*, 5 September 1856:5, 13 November 1851:2).

Smith's business operations were heavily criticised in *The Argus*. Seemingly, in the eyes of genteel Melbourne society, running neither a public house nor the Queen's Theatre were considered suitable occupations for a respectable man (De Serville 1991:209). Smith's hotels (Adelphi Hotel 1841–1844 and St John's Tavern 1844–1847) were occasionally at the centre of crime and scandal, but the reported incidents were rather minor (*Port Philip Patriot and Melbourne Advertiser*, 10 January 1842:2; *Port Philip Gazette*, 18 October 1843:2). When Smith wanted to ban skittles and quoits from being played at hotels, he was opposed by another publican who asserted that when Smith kept the Adelphi Hotel 'it was the most disgracefully conducted house in the whole colony, [and] that it was the receptacle of the most disreputable and disorderly characters'

(*Port Philip Gazette*, 7 September 1844:2). Certain performances at the Queen's Theatre also drew negative attention for their lack of respectability, but how much of this disreputable characterisation was reality as opposed to opinion is hard to say. There were also rumours that Smith was involved in running brothels (De Serville 1991:209). A cartoon (**Figure 43**) published in *Melbourne Punch* (1855, vol.1:78) depicts a farcical monument to Smith: a commentary on his possible involvement with

Figure 43: The Smith Monument, *Melbourne Punch* 1855 Vol.1, p.78 (Source: State Library of Victoria, www.slv.vic.gov.au).

prostitution and his lack of respectability. However, a careful comparison of Smith's property holdings (especially those in Niagara Lane) with newspaper reports of prosecutions and extant police records relating to prostitution in Melbourne produced no provable, or even hinted at, connections (PROV, VPRS 937/P0, Victoria Police Inward Registered Correspondence, Units 283–330; *The Argus*, 1848–1879).

Smith was accused of underhanded dealings on a number of occasions. In 1848 a letter to the editor implied that Smith forced his tenants and servants to vote for him (*The Argus*, 19 September 1848:2). Further, in 1850 Smith was accused of extorting money from the organisers of a benefit for the Benevolent Asylum (*The Argus*, 30 May 1850:4).

A letter to the editor appearing in *The Argus* in 1848 slammed Smith as lacking intelligence, ability and morals suggesting that he was only elected as Mayor because there was no-one better available in the colony at the time (*The Argus*, 19 September 1848:2). Three years later *The Argus* published this:

> Mr. Smith is, we have heard, a native of the colony, and as he is not now a young man, his years point to a period when New South Wales was a mere gaol, and the slightest vestiges of popular freedom were utterly unknown, simply because a community was not fit for them, which was mainly supplied with its component parts from the felonry of the mother-country. Reared amid such scenes, and the character moulded in such a school, what could be expected?...

> Mr. Smith has no single qualification for a useful public man, except a sort of dogged industry, and unbounded impudence; and these qualities are counter-balanced by as great failings as could well be embodied in a single individual. We point to his entire career as a public man in the City Council and elsewhere; and we assert that amongst the whole constituent portions of the new Legislative-representatives, nominees, and officials, there will not enter into that Chamber, one solitary individual who will prove such a thorough paced, uncompromising Government hack as this very gentleman (*The Argus*, 28 August 1851:2).

It is probably true that Smith would not have won the position of Mayor later in the century once Melbourne was established, and it ties in with broader social patterns and the peak of opportunity for social mobility in Melbourne which ran from the 1850s to 1880s (Cannon 1975:208).

The question of whether Smith was 'a gentleman' was of much concern. On the hustings in 1853 he quoted rival Lauchlan Mackinnon as having

come forward in the most brazen-faced manner and said that a tradesman was not honest enough, nor sufficiently a gentleman, to represent them in the Legislative Council (*Geelong Advertiser and Intelligencer*, 26 May 1853:1).

Rather than defending his honour as a gentleman, Smith turned the tables by proudly claiming his status as a tradesman, replying:

> If the matter at issue between himself and Mr Mackinnon were a question of ability, he, humble tradesman as he was, would back himself for odds, to discuss anything that might be proposed, and the present audience should be judges between them (*Geelong Advertiser and Intelligencer*, 26 May 1853:1).

He then played the class card in reverse:

> 'If they got a gentleman of such "gentility" to represent them,' he told the electors, 'the chances were, that he would cock his hat on one side, and not know them when they wanted to consult him' (*Geelong Advertiser and Intelligencer*, 26 May 1853:1).

The voting lists for 1853 (when he defeated Lauchlan Mackinnon for a Legislative Council seat for Melbourne) show that, in general, Smith was supported by the Irish and the publicans, but he was also supported by a number of wealthy, well-educated men as well as staunch tradesmen like himself, and prominent Jewish men. Redmond Barry does not appear on the 1851 voting list, but in the 1849 MCC election he also supported Smith (*The Argus*, 5 November 1849:2).

Smith helped frame Victoria's first constitution as a member of the earliest Legislative Councils. The constitution established election by secret ballot and a property qualification for the Legislative Council of 1856 (to be a member: £5000 property or £500 leasehold, and to vote: £1000 property or £100 leasehold). Smith was on the side of capital, but not of the landed gentry; he believed that men should earn the right of franchise through capital.

> They must have men of standing, – men who had raised themselves, if only to a bare competency, – such a man proved that he was respectable (*The Age*, 18 August 1856:6).

He wanted gold counted as property as well as land.

Politically, Smith was a conservative opportunist who valued capital and law and order (Serle 1963:259; Hayes 2017:2). Though conservative, he was not a conventionally educated or traditionally privileged conservative. He had a wide support base and his involvement with the Freemasons no doubt facilitated it by allowing him to develop networks with people from all walks of life (Hudson 2016).

Benevolence was clearly a priority for Smith. He believed that with wealth came responsibility and he initiated and funded the Melbourne Benevolent Asylum, campaigned for access to education (*The Age*, 18 August 1856:6), and handed out money to destitute people in the streets (*Bendigo Advertiser*, 31 January 1879:3).

His response to the Eureka uprising, however, was harsh and swift. Despite his sympathy for the working man, he was quick to erect strong boundaries to protect the status quo consistent with his concern with law and order (*The Age*, 18 August 1856:6; *The Argus*, 1 May 1857:5, 31 January 1879:6; *Bendigo Advertiser*, 31 January 1879:3; Serle 1963:112).

The sense I have of Smith is that he was a man deeply committed to his community, determined to succeed, highly practical, fond of a good time and not really too bothered about what people thought of him.

Ellen Smith's rags-to-riches tale is perhaps somewhat less dramatic. Ellen did not share Smith's convict heritage, but her Irish heritage, Roman Catholicism, and her father's occupation as a publican made her even less acceptable in the upper circles of Melbourne society than Smith. Ellen's marriage to Smith did not automatically give her the same status. A 'mixed marriage' (Catholic and Protestant) in this era brought with it something of the same discrimination as inter-racial marriages. An overt example of this discrimination is revealed in a letter from Governor Sir Henry Barkly, who wrote: 'Mrs Smith I have never invited to my Table, but on Public Occasions, have received her as the Mayor's Wife.' Smith was tolerated at the Governor's table but Ellen was not (De Serville 1991:209–211). Certainly an awkward social scenario.

Though never invited to dine at the Governor's house, Ellen was tolerated, if not accepted, elsewhere. She was one of the initial 19 women on the 'Ladies committee' for the Melbourne Lying-in Hospital (later the Royal Women's Hospital) (*The Argus*, 15 December 1856:5, 7 July 1860:1). So, like her husband, Ellen had benevolent attitudes and interests. Most of the other committee members were wives of Protestant clergymen, though, which is perhaps why Ellen's name did not appear more frequently with the committee.

The incident mentioned in the previous chapter, where Ellen and her sister-in-law Jane Smith helped themselves to goods from the shop of Jane's deceased brother-in-law Walker Barber is both evocative and telling. They chose silk and satin dresses, silk umbrellas, quality fabrics and 14 yards of merino. Jane also took family heirlooms, mainly her deceased sister's jewellery, from Barber's residence. In this period women could be trapped in marriage, with few work opportunities and oppressed by mothering and housework (see Lake 1988). Jane swore that the deceased had left the family jewellery to her and that she had been given permission to help herself to clothing from the shop. There was much conflicting testimony at the subsequent insolvency court proceeding as to what had been promised, what had been taken and what had later been charged to Smith (*The Argus*, 2 May 1856:5; *The Age*, 13 May 1856:3).

Had the women taken the window of opportunity while the men attended Barber's funeral to take more than they were entitled to? (Women did not attend funerals because of fear of them being unable to maintain composure (Russell 2010:254)). Maybe the women did have a legitimate claim to family jewellery and had no other recourse to obtain it? In any case, the Smiths were not found culpable by the court (*The Age*, 13 May 1856:3).

The Smiths' newly forged status benefitted the next generation. In adulthood, the Smiths' sons became barristers, medical practitioners and gentlemen squatters. The daughters married well – a superintendent of police, a barrister at law, an officer of police, a stock broker – and this was the predominant brand of success valued for middle-class women at this time. This is a remarkable move up from their convict grandparents.

THE SMITHS' BRAND OF CULTURAL CAPITAL

The above section addresses the social and economic capital of the family and what the trajectory of their lives reveals about their social status. However, as discussed in the introduction, the cultural capital of the family is of primary interest here and will now be examined, drawing on the previous chapters. Indicators against my definitions of respectability and gentility will be interrogated.

In my previous work on Viewbank homestead I argued that for the Martin family, gentility presented as an inherent quality that defined their position and also performed a distancing function to delineate the 'established middle class' from others seeking entry to their ranks (Hayes 2014:78). I argue here that 'aspirational early immigrants' like the Smiths would be appropriating cultural capital in their own distinctive ways for different purposes and that this would be reflected in their material culture.

I found three key indicators of gentility in the Viewbank assemblage: cohesion in high quality goods across all aspects of lifestyle; consistency in goods for both public and private use; and keeping up with fashions (Hayes 2008:286, 377–379, 2014:75). Here, variety, level of cohesion in public and private aspects, type of expensive or luxury goods and degree of fashion and good taste in the Queen Street assemblage are used to examine how the Smith family were using gentility and/or respectability as cultural capital. Evidence from the

Smiths' residence as a building and space will also be interrogated.

While some variety in the distribution of high quality goods in an assemblage is inevitable – think utilitarian mixing bowl versus fancy salt cellar – a distinctive distribution can be telling. In a working-class assemblage one might expect a large number of practical, cheap items with a handful of strategically chosen expensive or luxury items (Hayes 2014:75). In an 'established middle class' assemblage such as that at Viewbank, a consistent level of expense was noted with matching sets of both table and teaware, a variety of purpose-specific ceramic forms, high quality glassware, a large number of beverage bottles, expensive toys, personal items of luxury, medicine items and matching toilet sets (Hayes 2014:75). In the Queen Street assemblage the presence of expensive and luxury items indicates that the family had sufficient wealth to purchase such goods, but the distribution differs to that at Viewbank. While the wealth is clearly present in the Queen Street assemblage, greater expense was noted in the tableware than the teaware. There were both plain and highly decorated (but notably flawed) chamber pots.

Purchasing habits also play into this. The assemblage from Viewbank is suggestive of purchasing habits where desired goods could be bought in large numbers at one time in centralised arcades and specialised stores (as in the case of matching sets of ceramic or glass tableware). The Queen Street assemblage shows that the Smiths had the ability to purchase matching sets in a similar manner, but that they also utilised the seconds market for tableware and toiletware. The manor house at 300 Queen Street, as a sizeable piece of material culture, indicates much the same values as the assemblage itself. In particular, the extension added to the house was pretentious in nature but poorly executed (Nigel Lewis and Associates 1982:51).

Like the Martins (see Hayes 2014:75), the Smiths had a range of cheaper items for particular purposes such as use by the servants or for necessary household tasks. However, while there is no evidence in the Viewbank assemblage of scrimping and saving, at Queen Street there is some evidence of saving, such as use of the seconds market, and an expenditure emphasis on goods for public use (Hayes 2017).

Values around male/public and female/private spheres were important in the 19th century, as discussed in the previous chapter. The Smiths' best efforts and greatest expenditure were focused in areas of public display. The grand façade of the house at 300 Queen Street communicated status to the community at large: passersby could interpret the position of the occupants. The number of rooms and layout of the residence suggests that the Smith family had sufficient rooms to accommodate public and private spaces, and to segregate service areas from the main part of the house. The front of the house likely comprised the public rooms: dining room, drawing room and hall. These three public rooms served the specific functions of receiving, eating and entertaining (Young 2003:175). Visitors were received in these rooms without access or exposure to the private areas of the house. Public rooms communicated the success and status of the occupants, and generally the greatest expense went into fitting and furnishing them (Flanders 2003:xxv, xxviii). The front section of the home was quite separate from the private sleeping and service areas behind. This demarcation between the public areas and the private rooms for the family members was important, as was separation of both of these areas from the rooms for servants (Flanders 2003:xxv). At 300 Queen Street, bedrooms were situated upstairs, and service areas most likely in the basement, out of sight and private.

Dining was a vital area of public display for the middle class in the 19th-century. The presentation of meals at 300 Queen Street was showy and colourful. For the influential men of early Melbourne dining was an important arena for networking. An invitation to dine at the Governor's table implied a certain level of social acceptance and when Smith invited the Governor to dine with him (De Serville 1991:211) I can imagine a certain amount of consideration went into the choice of tableware.

When compared to the Viewbank tableware, the vessels used at Queen Street were more elaborate with more cases of multiple decoration types, and were, dare I say, more gaudy. At first I was tempted to interpret this as suggesting the Smiths' desire to impress their dinner guests with the multiple highly decorated sets in the cesspit a result of anxiety over appearances and constantly updating their choice of tableware. But, this does not quite fit with the rest of the picture emerging regarding the Smiths' cultural capital. There is a potent lack of concern with what the upper crust thought of them coming through the historical records. The showy ceramics suggest, I am more inclined to think, a desire to display wealth and a liking for gaudy colours but not a concern with gaining entry to the 'established middle class'.

The teawares at Queen Street were dominated by single colour flow and transfer-printed teaware: decidedly less showy than the tableware. This was not the case at Viewbank where the teawares were dominated by gilt and multiple decorations (Hayes 2014:33–34). I am inclined to interpret the more demure teaware at Queen Street as suggesting that the Smiths placed less priority on their teaware purchases. We know from the historical records that Ellen was not fully accepted by the elite and perhaps not a part of the circle of receiving and paying calls. Formalised calls were really the domain of the 'established middle class' and perhaps, among women from the 'early aspiration immigrants' calls were not as important or did not require special teaware.

Ceramics for use in the private areas of 300 Queen Street were generally cheaper and less showy. Food preparation and storage items were strictly utilitarian. There were no matching toilet sets for use in the bedrooms. The three chamber pots recovered suggest that this was not an arena of priority for expenditure. One was flow transfer floral pattern, another unadorned whiteware and a third was a transfer-printed classical scene. The chamber pot with the image of Athena was showy but had very obvious flaws in the placement of the transfer suggesting that in the private area they still liked showy things, but were not altogether concerned with their quality. This contrasts to Viewbank where matching sets and elaborate decorations extended into private toiletwares.

This leads in to a consideration of fashions at 300 Queen Street. As discussed in the previous chapter, the degree of completeness of many of the ceramics discarded in the cesspit might indicate a desire to keep up with fashions. The pattern of showy, elaborate display present in the tableware and the manor house can also be seen in aspects of the Smiths' personal appearances. His white top hat (**Figure 12**) undoubtedly set him apart and, in my mind, expressed his wealth and power along with his lack of interest in conformity. The Barber affair and Ellen's underhanded acquisition of fine fabrics – silk, merino wool – indicate her interest in finery. But the over-the-top display of wealth in fashion of families like the Smiths was not considered tasteful among the colonial elite.

The Smiths had different ideas about fashion to the Martins' quietly refined taste (Hayes 2017). The material culture at 300 Queen Street does not fit with 19th-century concepts of appropriate spending: not too little, not too much (Young 2003:88–91; Hayes 2014:55). Fashion for the Smiths was showy, gaudy and inaccurate by the genteel standards of Melbourne at the time, suggesting to me that fashions for the Smiths were less about fitting in and more about showing off.

The pattern of origins of goods discarded by the Smiths was also quite distinct from the Martins (Hayes 2014:58, 2017:10). There is a notable lack of exotic luxury goods such as French champagne and imports from Asian countries at Queen Street. While it is important to note that English-manufactured goods do not necessarily indicate English values or beliefs (Symonds 2003:153), the Smith family may well have sought English goods as an element of cultural capital. In conjunction with this, the absence of Irish goods in spite of Ellen Smith's Irish heritage, might suggest a purposeful step away from her past (see Brighton 2011:45 for a similar arguement).

The Smiths adapted and appropriated respectability and gentility in their own particular ways. To recap the definitions I am working with here, respectability was determined primarily through possessions and deeds, not predetermined by familial status or upbringing, and was strategic in nature with a strong emphasis on materialism, while gentility was defensive in nature with an emphasis on protecting status, and determined by upbringing and manner which cannot be copied or appropriated (Hayes 2017:6–7). Against my definitions it can be seen that the Smiths selected and adapted aspects of both brands of cultural capital. In the absence of a familial claim to the middle class, the family placed an exaggerated emphasis on possessions. They used their consumption to display their wealth and pronounce their success. Their actions and manners, however, do not appear from the newspapers of the day as entirely respectable with underhanded dealings and morally questionable goings on. This is a major way in which I see that the Smiths engaged differently with respectability to the working class. The working class were in some cases deeply concerned with actions, behaviour and manners in order to announce themselves as respectable and enable opportunities for social mobility in the absence of wealth (Karskens and Lawrence 2003:98). The Smiths had their wealth and as such were more concerned with possessions. Respectability, for the working class and the Smiths alike, was frequently strategic: to improve financial or social position, to gain entry to a higher social class. However, this was not a simple matter of emulation. The Smiths' strategy was not to emulate and be accepted by the 'established middle class' but to be successful by their own and newly formed social measures (more on this in the next section). There is much potential to further interrogate working-class uses of respectability and instances where respectability was not about social mobility (Karskens 1997:230–232), but the focus here is on the middle class.

Aspects of gentility based on upbringing and manner were beyond the reach of the Smiths. Bourdieu (1977) argues that the primary transmission of cultural capital is from parent to child, and as such the Smiths missed out on this inherent aspect of gentility. Yet, I argue that they still engaged with it. Their manor house is the most obvious example: Georgian in style and outdated in the Australian context, the house gave the family the impression of heritage and being from 'old money'. Displaying wealth, a vital aspect of gentility (Hayes 2014:51), was clearly important to the Smiths but took on a gaudy, over-the-top aspect that would never be a part of the 'established middle-class' brand of gentility. The restraint and refined taste notable in the Viewbank assemblage is absent at Queen Street.

I argued previously (Hayes 2014:78) that the Martins used gentility to differentiate and delineate themselves from those seeking entry to their ranks.

The Smiths are the perfect example of the type of people the Martins were trying to keep out. Yet, this delineating aspect of gentility was also present in the Smiths' cultural capital. By having the wealth to display status through possessions the Smiths delineated themselves from others with similar backgrounds who had not successfully transitioned into the middle class.

The Smiths' use of gentility and respectability as cultural capital was not a simple matter of emulating the middle class in order to gain entry, nor was it purely a social strategy. It was in part a refashioning of the society around them.

Redefining the Middle Class

Tensions between the 'established middle class' and the 'aspirational early immigrants' led to significant changes to the middle class in the colony of Victoria. From the very beginnings of European settlement the necessity of accepting families like the Smiths into the middle class and handing over social power in the form of important public roles to such people caused much consternation (Russell 2002:435).

The small numbers of 'established middle class' families in Victoria meant that important public roles had to be filled by up-and-coming people. Government, council, associations, charities etc. all grew to rely on the contributions of the newly rich. In the earliest years the demand enabled the rapid social mobility of many. If Smith had arrived in the colony later in the century it is unlikely that he would have become Mayor (Hayes 2017).

Yet tensions remained. As Russell (2010:122) points out, 'admission to Government House defined the boundaries of "good society"', and while John Thomas Smith gained admittance his wife, Ellen, did not. The tentative acceptance of the Smiths in the colony by no means translated to the mother country. John Thomas Smith travelled to England in 1858 to present an address on behalf of the Melbourne City Council on the occasion of the Princess Royal's marriage. While there, Smith hoped that he would receive a knighthood, commonplace for Mayors of major British outposts, and carried with him a testimonial from various Melbourne dignitaries. However, he was sabotaged by rumours about his character and Edward Wilson of *The Argus* felt so strongly that he followed Smith to England with the express purpose of sullying his name. Smith did not receive the honour (De Serville 1991:209–210). It was an embarrassing affair, not just for Smith but for all of Melbourne. Though insulted, at the same time the Governor, Sir Henry Barkly, noted that 'in these Colonies Knighthood is the highest and sole order of nobility, and the Judges and Presidents, who are really Gentlemen, will deem it little compliment to have their honours shared by Sir John and Lady Smith' (De Serville 1991:210). It was an insult to Melbourne but a relief for the elite.

The 'aspirational early immigrants' gradually became the bigger group within Melbourne's middle class. Outnumbered, the 'established middle class' began to decline (Hayes 2017:13–14). The pretensions of the highest levels of society were often poked fun at by the newly rich, and English manners, so important to the 'established middle class', were considered 'absurd remnants of the "old world"' to self-made Australians (Russell 2002:431). Within this context, Smith was successful in capitalising on his position in society, and while the Martins did not fail as such, their influence and position was diminished by the upcoming aspirational group. The fact that John Thomas Smith was not completely accepted by the 'established middle class' did not really matter. In the words of contemporary diarist Clara Aspinall 'the rich were rarely gentlemen, the gentlemen rarely rich' (De Serville 1991:21).

This is echoed in the material culture. The Smiths were keen to enjoy their success with showy, gaudy displays of wealth. Their cultural capital was not about fitting in but about forging their own new path. As Bourdieu (1977, 1984) argues, a pivotal determining factor in an individual's judgement of their class is cultural capital, and the Smiths were taking the opportunity provided by the new colony to reinvent theirs. The use of consumer goods was part of shaping and redefining the middle class and what was accepted. I see this as the Smiths using cultural capital as a tactic to push social boundaries and improve their position.

Conclusion

The Smith family evoke the turmoil, volatility and opportunity of life in the first decades of the colony of Port Phillip. They provide an example of the possibility of social mobility in the colony, but also of the difficulty of navigating the customs and foibles of a newly forming society. In spite of the Smiths' best efforts to communicate status through material culture, and their undeniable wealth and success, they remained outside of genteel 'established middle class' Melbourne society. However, and more importantly, they were reinventing what class meant in Melbourne. Material culture and the distinctive engagement with gentility and respectability of the Smiths was part of a new cultural capital that ultimately redefined the middle class in Melbourne.

As Mayor, John Thomas Smith had the power to sculpt society. The tactics he used were, to some extent, constrained by society but he pushed the boundaries and influenced the social structure around him. He wanted to be noticed not in a way that fitted with the demure, 'established middle class', but to improve his position. Such tactics went hand-in-hand with the emerging multiplicity of Melbourne's middle class which became a highly varied group.

The circumstances of new settlement and the numerical dominance of 'aspirational early immigrants' gave this group a newly heightened power over what mattered with regard to cultural capital in Melbourne. The Smiths picked and chose from respectability and gentility to further themselves, rather than to be accepted. John Thomas Smith could afford socially, financially and culturally to be an oddity. It seems to me that he succeeded and he enjoyed it.

Works Cited

ARCHIVAL SOURCES

Archives Office of Tasmania

Reports of Ships Arrivals with Lists of Passengers, Film Number SLTX/AO/MB/1, Series Number MB2/39/1/1

Land Use Victoria General Law Library, Laverton (LUV GLL)

Old Law Memorials and Deeds, First and Second Series Indexes

National Archives (UK)

1911 England Census Essex, Wivenhoe, District 199, Class: RG14; Piece: 10333; Schedule Number: 268

1911 England Census London, Strand, District 13, Class: RG14; Piece: 1196

Home Office, Convict Prison Hulks: Registers and Letter Books; Class: HO9; Piece: 4

Public Record Office of Victoria

VA 724 Victoria Police, VPRS 937/P0 Inward Registered Correspondence, Units 283–330

VA 865 Department of the Treasurer, VPRS 7/P0 Inward Correspondence (Bound), Index to inward correspondence regarding publicans 1838–1855

VA 511 Melbourne (Town 1842–1847; City 1847–ct), VPRS 5702/P0 Bourke Ward Rate Books 1847–1864

VA 511 Melbourne (Town 1842–1847; City 1847–ct), VPRS 5708/P9 Rate Books 1861–1888

VA 2624 Master in Equity, VPRS 28/P0 Unit 393, Ellen Smith

VA 2624 Master in Equity, VPRS 28/P2 Unit 89 John Thomas Smith

VA 2624 Master in Equity, VPRS 7591/P2, Unit 46 John Thomas Smith

State Archives New South Wales (SANSW)

1828 NSW Census (Australian copy) Householders' returns Surnames L-T NRS 1272

National Library of Australia, TROVE Newspapers online

The Age 1855–1856

The Argus 1848–1927

The Australian News for Home Readers 1864

Bendigo Advertiser 1879

Geelong Advertiser 1848–1859

Geelong Advertiser and Intelligencer 1853

Leader 1863

The Melbourne Argus 1847

The Port Phillip Gazette 1843–1844

Port Phillip Gazette and Settler's Journal 1847

Port Phillip Herald 1848

Port Phillip Patriot and Melbourne Advertiser 1842

Punch 1855

REFERENCES

Adams, W.H. 1991, Trade Networks and Interaction Spheres – A View from Silcott. In G. L. Miller, O. R. Jones, L. A. Ross and T. Majewski (eds.) *Approaches to Material Culture Research for Historical Archaeologists*, Society for Historical Archaeology, Pennsylvania, pp. 385–398.

Allison, P.M. and A. Cremin 2006, Ceramics from the Old Kinchega Homestead. *Australasian Historical Archaeology*, 24: 55–64.

Ames, K.L. 1978, Meaning in Artifacts: Hall Furnishings in Victorian America. *Journal of Interdisciplinary History*, 9(1): 19–46.

Annear, R. 1995, *Bearbrass: Imagining Early Melbourne*. Mandarin, Melbourne.

Appadurai, A. (ed.) 1986, *The Social Life of Things: Commodities in Cultural Perspective*. Cambridge University Press, Cambridge.

Architects' Emergency Committee 1970, *Great Georgian Houses of America: Published for the Benefit of the Architects' Emergency Committee*, Vol. 1. Dover Publications, New York.

Aspinall, C. 1862, *Three Years in Melbourne*. L. Booth, London.

Attwood, B. 2009, *Possession: Batman's Treaty and the Matter of History*. Miegunyah Press, Melbourne.

Barile, K.S. and J. C. Brandon (eds.) 2004, *Household Chores and Household Choices: Theorizing the Domestic Sphere in Historical Archaeology*. University of Alabama Press, Alabama.

Barnard, M. 1963, The Georgian Context: New South Wales. In M. Dupain (ed.) *Georgian*

Architecture in Australia: With Some Examples of Buildings of the Post-Georgian Period, Ure Smith, Sydney.

Beaudry, M. 2006, *Findings: The Material Culture of Needlework and Sewing*. Yale University Press, New Haven.

Beeston, J. 1994, *A Concise History of Australian Wine*. Allen & Unwin, Sydney.

Beeton, I.M. 1861, *Beeton's Book of Household Management*. S. O. Beeton, London.

Birmingham, J. 1990, A Decade of Digging: Deconstructing Urban Archaeology. *Australian Historical Archaeology*, 8: 13–22.

Birmingham, J. 1992, *Wybalenna: The Archaeology of Cultural Accommodation in Nineteenth Century Tasmania*. Australian Society for Historical Archaeology, Sydney.

Blanton, R.E. 1994, *Houses and Households: A Comparative Study*. Plenum Press, New York.

Bourdieu, P. 1977, *Outline of a Theory of Practice*. Translated by R. Nice, Cambridge University Press, Cambridge.

Bourdieu, P. 1984, *Distinction: A Social Critique of the Judgment of Taste*. Harvard University Press, Cambridge, Massachusetts.

Boyce, J. 2011, *1835: The Founding of Melbourne & the Conquest of Australia*. Black Inc., Melbourne.

Brighton, S.A. 2011, Middle-Class Ideologies and American Respectability: Archaeology and the Irish Immigrant Experience. *International Journal of Historical Archaeology*, 15(1): 30–50.

Broadbent, J. 1995, *Elizabeth Farm Parramatta: A History and a Guide*. Historic Houses Trust of New South Wales, Sydney.

Brooks, A. 2005, *An Archaeological Guide to British Ceramics in Australia 1788–1901*. Australasian Society for Historical Archaeology and the La Trobe University Archaeology Program, Sydney.

Brooks, A. 2010, A Not So Useless Beauty: Economy, Status, Function, and Meaning in the Interpretation of Transfer-Printed Tablewares. In J. Symonds (ed.) *Table Settings: The Material Culture and Social Context of Dining Ad 1700–1900*, Oxbow, Oxford, pp. 154–162.

Broome, R. 1984, *The Victorians: Arriving*. Fairfax Series, Fairfax, Syme & Weldon Associates, Sydney.

Broome, R. 2005, *Aboriginal Victorians: A History Since 1800*. Allen & Unwin, Sydney.

Brown-May, A. 1998, *Melbourne Street Life*. Australian Scholarly Publishing, Melbourne.

Busch, J. 1991, Second Time Around: A Look at Bottle Reuse. In G. L. Miller, O. R. Jones, L. A. Ross and T. Majewski (eds.) *Approaches to Material Culture Research for Historical Archaeologists*, Society for Historical Archaeology, Pennsylvania, pp. 113–126.

Bushman, R. 1993, *The Refinement of America: Persons, Houses, Cities*. Vintage Books, New York.

Campbell, J. 2002, *Invisible Invaders: Smallpox and Other Diseases in Aboriginal Australia 1780–1880*. Melbourne University Press, Melbourne.

Cannon, M. 1966, *The Land Boomers*. Cambridge University Press, Cambridge.

Cannon, M. 1971, *Australia in the Victorian Age: Who's Master? Who's Man?*. John Currey O'Neil, Melbourne.

Cannon, M. 1974, Munro, David (1844–1898). In *Australian Dictionary of Biography*, Melbourne University Press, Melbourne, Vol. 5, pp. 311–312.

Cannon, M. 1975, *Australia in the Victorian Age 3: Life in the Cities*. Thomas Nelson Australia, Melbourne.

Carlin, S. 2000, *Elizabeth Bay House: A History & Guide*. Historic Houses Trust of New South Wales, Sydney.

Carney, M. 1998, A Cordial Factory at Parramatta, New South Wales. *Australasian Historical Archaeology*, 16: 80–93.

Casella, E.C. and S.K. Croucher 2010, *The Alderley Sandhills Project: An Archaeology of Community Life in (Post-) Industrial England*. Manchester University Press, Manchester.

Casey, M. 2005, Material Culture and the Construction of Hierarchy at the Conservatorium Site, Sydney. *Australasian Historical Archaeology*, 23: 97–113.

Colligan, M. 2005, Queen's Theatre. In A. Brown-May and S. Swain (eds.) *The Encyclopedia of Melbourne*, Cambridge University Press, Port Melbourne, p. 583.

G.M.H. Consultants 1999, The Cumberland/Gloucester Streets Site, The Rocks: Archaeological Investigation Report. Report submitted to the Sydney Cove Authority, Sydney.

Crook, P. 2000, Shopping and Historical Archaeology: Exploring the Contexts of Urban Consumption. *Australasian Historical Archaeology*, 18: 17–28.

Crook, P. 2005, Quality, Cost and Value: Key Concepts for an Interpretive Assemblage Analysis. *Australasian Historical Archaeology*, 23: 15–24.

Crook, P. 2008, 'Superior Quality': Exploring the Nature of Cost, Quality and Value in Historical Archaeology. Unpublished PhD thesis, La Trobe University, Melbourne.

Crook, P. 2011, Rethinking Assemblage Analysis: New Approaches to the Archaeology of Working-Class Neighborhoods. *International Journal of Historical Archaeology*, 15(4): 582–593.

Crook, P., L. Ellmoos and T. Murray 2003, *Assessment of Historical and Archaeological Resources of the Cumberland and Gloucester Streets site, The Rocks, Sydney*. Archaeology of the Modern City 1788–1900 Series, Volume 3, Historic Houses Trust of New South Wales, Sydney.

Crook, P., L. Ellmoos and T. Murray 2005, *Keeping Up with the McNamaras: A Historical Archaeological Study of the Cumberland and Gloucester Streets Site, The Rocks, Sydney*. Archaeology of the Modern City 1788–1900 Series, Volume 8, Historic Houses Trust of New South Wales, Sydney.

Crook, P., L. Ellmoos and T. Murray 2006a, *Exploring the Archaeology of the Modern City Project Databases*. Archaeology of the Modern City 1788–1900 Series, Volume 13, Historic Houses Trust of New South Wales, Sydney.

Crook, P., L. Ellmoos and T. Murray 2006b, *People+Place: A Guide to Using the Database*. Archaeology of the Modern City 1788–1900 Series, Volume 9, Historic Houses Trust of New South Wales, Sydney.

Crook, P., S. Lawrence and M. Gibbs 2002, The Role of Artefact Catalogues in Australian Historical Archaeology: A Framework for Discussion. *Australasian Historical Archaeology*, 20: 26–38.

Crook, P. and T. Murray 2004, The Analysis of Cesspit Deposits from the Rocks, Sydney. *Australasian Historical Archaeology*, 22: 44–56.

Crook, P. and T. Murray 2006, *Guide to the EAMC Archaeology Database*. Archaeology of the Modern City 1788–1900 Series, Volume 10, Historic Houses Trust of New South Wales, Sydney.

Davey, P. (ed.) 1987, *The Archaeology of the Clay Tobacco Pipe: X. Scotland*. BAR British Series 178, Oxford.

Davidoff, L. and C. Hall 2002, *Family Fortunes: Men and Women of the English Middle Class, 1780–1850*. Routledge, London.

Davies, P. 2001, A Cure for All Seasons: Health and Medicine in a Bush Community. *Journal of Australian Studies*, 70: 63–72.

Davies, P. 2004, Glass and Stoneware Containers. Unpublished report to the ISPT and Heritage Victoria, Melbourne.

Davies, P. 2005, Writing Slates and Schooling. *Australasian Historical Archaeology*, 23: 63–69.

Davies, P. 2006, Mapping Commodities at Casselden Place. *International Journal of Historical Archaeology*, 10(4): 343–355.

Davison, G. 1978, *The Rise and Fall of Marvellous Melbourne*. Melbourne University Press, Melbourne.

Davison, G. 2000, Colonial Origins of the Australian Home. In P. Troy (ed.) *A History of European Housing in Australia*, Cambridge University Press, Cambridge, pp. 6–25.

De Serville, P. 1991, *Pounds and Pedigrees: The Upper Class in Victoria 1850–1880*. Oxford University Press, Melbourne.

Deutsher, K.M. 1999, *The Breweries of Australia: A History*. Lothian Books, Melbourne.

Dingle, T. 1984, *The Victorians: Settling*. Fairfax, Syme & Weldon Associates, Sydney.

Douglas, M. and B. Isherwood 1978, *The World of Goods: Towards an Anthropology of Consumption*. Penguin Books, Ringwood.

Dunstan, D. 1994, *Better Than Pommard! A History of Wine In Victoria*. Australian Scholarly Publishing and Museum Victoria, Melbourne.

Eastwood, J. 1976, Smith, John Thomas (1816–1879). In *Australian Dictionary of Biography*, Melbourne University Press, Melbourne, Vol. 6, pp. 150–151.

Ellis, A. 2001, Toy Stories: Interpreting Childhood from the Victorian Archaeological Record. Unpublished Honours thesis, La Trobe University, Melbourne.

Ellis, A. and B. Woff 2017, Bottle Merchants at A'Beckett Street, Melbourne (1875–1914): New Evidence for the Light Industrial Trade of Bottle Washing. *International Journal of Historical Archaeology*, Online first (May): 1–21.

Finn, E. 1888, *The Chronicles of Early Melbourne, 1835 to 1852: Historical, Anecdotal and Personal by "Garryowen"*. Fergusson and Mitchell, Melbourne.

Fitts, R. 1999, The Archaeology of Middle-Class Domesticity and Gentility in Victorian Brooklyn. *Historical Archaeology*, 33(1): 39–62.

Flanders, J. 2003, *The Victorian House: Domestic Life from Childbirth to Deathbed*. Harper Collins, London.

Ford, G. 1995, *Australian Pottery: The First 100 Years*. Salt Glaze Press, Wodonga.

Friedman, J. 1994, *Consumption and Identity*. Studies in Anthropology and History, Harwood Academic, Switzerland.

Gaynor, A. 2005, Food, Suburban Production. In A. Brown-May and S. Swain (eds.) *The Encyclopedia of Melbourne*, Cambridge University Press, Melbourne, pp. 277–278.

Gibb, J. 1996, *The Archaeology of Wealth: Consumer Behaviour in English America*. Plenum Press, New York.

Giddens, A. 1973, *The Class Structure of Advanced Societies*. Hutchinson University Library, London.

Giddens, A. 1984, *The Constitution of Society: Outline of the Theory of Structuration*. Polity Press, Cambridge.

Glassie, H. 1975, *Folk Housing in Middle Virginia: A Structural Analysis of Historic Artefacts*. University of Tennessee Press, Knoxville.

Godden, G. 1964, *Encyclopaedia of British Pottery and Porcelain Marks*. Barrie & Jenkins, London.

Godden Mackay Logan, Austral Archaeology and La Trobe University 2004, Casselden Place, 50 Lonsdale Street, Melbourne, Archaeological Excavations Research Archive Report, Volume 2: Trench Reports. Report to the ISPT and Heritage Victoria, Melbourne.

Gojak, D. and I. Stuart 1999, The Potential for the Archaeological Study of Clay Tobacco Pipes from Australian Sites. *Australasian Historical Archaeology*, 17: 38–49.

Goodwin, L.B.R. 1999, *An Archaeology of Manners: The Polite World of the Merchant Elite of Colonial Massachusetts*. Kluwer Academic/Plenum Press, New York.

Graham, K. 2005, The Archaeological Potential of Medicinal Advertisements. *Australasian Historical Archaeology*, 23: 47–53.

Graham, M. 1981, *Australian Glass of the 19th and Early 20th Century*. David Ell Press, Sydney.

Griffin, R. 2004, Fireplaces. In Historic Houses Trust of New South Wales (ed.) *The Art of Keeping House: A Practical and Inspirational Guide*, Hardie Grant Books, Melbourne, pp. 48–55.

Hagger, J. 1979, *Australian Colonial Medicine*. Rigby, Adelaide.

Hayes, S. 2007, Consumer Practice at Viewbank Homestead. *Australasian Historical Archaeology*, 25: 87–103.

Hayes, S. 2008, Being Middle Class: An Archaeology of Gentility in Nineteenth-Century Australia. Unpublished PhD thesis, La Trobe University, Melbourne.

Hayes, S. 2011a, Amalgamation of Archaeological Assemblages: Experiences from the Commonwealth Block Project, Melbourne. *Australian Archaeology*, 73: 13–24.

Hayes, S. 2011b, Gentility in the Dining and Tea Service Practices of Early Colonial Melbourne's "Established Middle Class". *Australasian Historical Archaeology*, 29: 33–44.

Hayes, S. 2011c, A Historical Archaeology of the Commonwealth Block 1850–1950: Artefact Processing Project Report. Report to the La Trobe University and Museum Victoria, Melbourne.

Hayes, S. 2014, *Good Taste, Fashion, Luxury: A Genteel Melbourne Family and Their Rubbish*. Studies in Australasian Historical Archaeology 5, Sydney University Press, Sydney.

Hayes, S. 2017, A Golden Opportunity: Mayor Smith and Melbourne's Emergence as a Global City. *International Journal of Historical Archaeology*, Online First: 1–17.

Hayes, S. and B. Minchinton 2016, Cesspit Formation Processes and Waste Management History in Melbourne: Evidence from Little Lon. *Australian Archaeology*, 82(1): 12–24.

Herman, M. 1963, The Architecture and the Architects. In M. Dupain (ed.) *Georgian Architecture in Australia: With Some Examples of Buildings of the Post-Georgian Period*, Ure Smith, Sydney.

Hetherington, J. 1964, *Witness to Things Past: Stone, Brick, Wood and Men in Early Victoria*. F. W. Cheshire, Melbourne.

Higman, B.W. 2002, *Domestic Service in Australia*. Melbourne University Press, Melbourne.

Hirst, J. 1988, Egalitarianism. In S.L. Goldberg and F. B. Smith (eds.) *Australian Cultural History*, Cambridge University Press, Cambridge, pp. 58–77.

Hocking, G. 2004, *Eureka Stockade: A Pictorial History: The Events Leading to the Attack in the Pre-Dawn of 3 December 1854*. Five Mile Press, Rowville.

Hourani, P. 1990, Spatial Organisation and the Status of Women in Nineteenth Century Australia. *Australian Historical Archaeology*, 8: 70–77.

Hudson, D. 2016, Famous and/or Notable Australian Freemasons. Retrieved 20 March 2016 from http://www.lodgedevotion.net/devotionnews/education-editorial-articles/famous-australian-freemasons/large-list-of-notable-and-famous-australian-freemasons#_Toc439263603.

Iacono, N. 1999, Miscellaneous Artefacts Reports. The Cumberland/Gloucester Streets Site, The Rocks: Archaeological Investigation Report, Volume 4, Part 2, Godden Mackay Heritage Consultants, Report submitted to the Sydney Cove Authority, Sydney, pp. 11–118.

Jones, O. 2000, A Guide to Dating Glass Tableware: 1800 to 1940. In K. Karklins (ed.) *Studies in Material Culture Research*, Society for Historical Archaeology, Pennsylvania, pp. 141–232.

Karskens, G. 1997, *The Rocks: Life in Early Sydney*. Melbourne University Press, Melbourne.

Karskens, G. 1999, *Inside the Rocks: The Archaeology of a Neighbourhood*. Hale and Iremonger, Sydney.

Karskens, G. 2001, Small Things, Big Pictures: New Perspectives from the Archaeology of Sydney's Rocks Neighbourhood. In A. Mayne and T. Murray (eds.) *The Archaeology of Urban Landscapes: Explorations in Slumland*, New Directions in Archaeology Series, University of Cambridge, Cambridge, pp. 69–85.

Karskens, G. and S. Lawrence 2003, The Archaeology of Cities: What Is It We Want to Know?. In T. Murray (ed.) *Exploring the Modern City: Recent Approaches to Urban History and Archaeology*, Historic Houses Trust of New South Wales in association with La Trobe University, Sydney, pp. 89–111.

Kent, S. 1990, *Domestic Architecture and the Use of Space: An Interdisciplinary Cross-Cultural Study*. Cambridge University Press, New York.

King, L. and N. King 1982, Franklin House, Tasmania. In *Historic Houses*, Australian Council of National Trusts, Canberra.

Kingston, B. 1994, *Basket, Bag and Trolley: A History of Shopping in Australia*. Oxford University Press, Melbourne.

Knehans, M.M. 2005, The Archaeology and History of Pharmacy in Victoria. *Australasian Historical Archaeology*, 23: 41–46.

Kociumbas, J. 1992, *Possessions 1770–1860*, The Oxford History of Australia, Volume 2, Oxford University Press Australia, Melbourne.

Kociumbas, J. 1997, *Australian Childhood: A History*. Allen & Unwin, Sydney.

Lake, M. 1988, Intimate Strangers. In V. Burgmann and J. Lee (eds.) *Making a Life*, A People's History of Australia Since 1788 series, McPhee Gribble, Melbourne.

Lampard, S. 2004, Urban Living: The Respectable of Jane Street, Port Adelaide. In D. Arthur and A. Paterson (eds.) *National Archaeology Students Conference: Explorations, Investigations and New Directions*, National Archaeology Students Conference, Adelaide, pp. 26–32.

Lampard, S. 2009, The Ideology of Domesticity and the Working-Class Women and Children of Port Adelaide, 1840–1880. *Historical Archaeology*, 43(3): 50–64.

Lampard, S. and M. Staniforth 2011, The Demon Drink: Working-Class Attitudes to Alcohol in Nineteenth-Century Port Adelaide. *Australasian Historical Archaeology*, 29: 5–12.

Lane, T. and J. Serle 1990, *Australians at Home: A Documentary History of Australian Domestic Interiors from 1788 to 1914*. Oxford University Press, Melbourne.

Lawrence, S. 1998, The Role of Material Culture in Australasian Archaeology. *Australasian Historical Archaeology*, 16: 8–15.

Lawrence, S. 2000, *Dolly's Creek: An Archaeology of a Victorian Goldfields Community*. Melbourne University Press, Melbourne.

Lawrence, S. 2003, Exporting Culture: Archaeology and the Nineteenth-Century British Empire. *Historical Archaeology*, 37(1): 20–33.

Lawrence, S. 2006, *Whalers and Free Men: Life on Tasmania's Colonial Whaling Stations*. Australian Scholarly, Melbourne.

Lawrence, S., A. Brooks and J. Lennon 2009, Ceramics and Status in Regional Australia. *Australasian Historical Archaeology*, 27: 67–78.

Lawrence, S. and P. Davies 2011, *An Archaeology of Australia Since 1788*. Springer, New York.

Lawrence, S. and P. Davies 2015, Innovation, Adaptation and Technology as Habitus: The Origins of Alluvial Gold Mining Methods in Australia. *Archaeology in Oceania*, 50: 20–29.

Lewis, M. 1985, The Victorian House. In R. Irving (ed.) *The History & Design of the Australian House*, Oxford University Press, Melbourne.

Lindbergh, J. 1999, Buttoning Down Archaeology. *Australasian Historical Archaeology*, 17: 50–57.

Lindsey, B. 2011, Historic Glass Bottle Identification and Information Website. Retrieved from www.sha.org/bottle/.

Lydon, J. 1993a, Archaeology in The Rocks, Sydney, 1979–1993: From Old Sydney Gaol to Mrs Lewis' Boarding-House. *Australasian Historical Archaeology*, 11: 33–42.

Lydon, J. 1993b, Task Differentiation in Historical Archaeology: Sewing as Material Culture. In H. du Cros and L. Smith (eds.) *Women in Archaeology: A Feminist Critique*, Department of Prehistory, Research School of Pacific Studies, Australian National University, Canberra, pp. 129–133.

Lydon, J. 1998, Boarding-Houses in The Rocks: Mrs Ann Lewis' Privy 1865. In M. Casey, D. Donlon, J. Hope and S. Wellfare (eds.) *Redefining Archaeology: Feminist Perspectives*, ANH Publications, Canberra, pp. 138–144.

Lydon, J. 1999, *Many Inventions: The Chinese in The Rocks 1890–1930*. Monash Publications in History, Melbourne.

Majewski, T. and M. B. Schiffer 2001, Beyond Consumption: Toward an Archaeology of Consumption. In V. Buchli and G. Lucas (eds.) *Archaeologies of the Contemporary Past*, Routledge, London, pp. 26–50.

Marsden, G. 1998, Introduction. In G. Marsden (ed.) *Victorian Values: Personalities and Perspectives in Nineteenth-Century Society*, Longman, London.

Matthews, C. N. 2010, *The Archaeology of American Capitalism*. University Press of Florida, Gainesville.

Maynard, M. 1994, *Fashioned from Penury: Dress as Cultural Practice in Colonial Australia*. Cambridge University Press, Cambridge.

Mayne, A. and S. Lawrence 1998, An Ethnography of Place: Imagining "Little Lon". *Journal of Australian Studies*, 57: 93–107.

McCarthy, J. 1989, Archaeological Investigation: Commonwealth Offices and Telecom Corporate Building Sites, The Commonwealth Block, Melbourne, Victoria, Volume 1: Historical and Archaeological Report. Report to the Department of Administrative Services and Telecom Australia by Austral Archaeology, Melbourne.

McCarthy, P. 2001, Values and Identity in the "Working-Class" Worlds of Late Nineteenth-Century Minneapolis. In A. Mayne and T. Murray (eds.) *The Archaeology of Urban Landscapes: Explorations in Slumland*, New Directions in Archaeology Series, University of Cambridge, Cambridge, pp. 145–153.

McCracken, G. 1988, *Culture and Consumption: New Approaches to the Symbolic Character of Consumer Goods and Activities*. Indiana University Press, Indianapolis.

McKendrick, N., J. Brewer and O.H. Plumb 1982, *The Birth of Consumer Society: The Commercialization of Eighteenth-Century England*. Indiana University Press, Indianapolis.

Miller, D. 1987, *Material Culture and Mass Consumption*. Basil Blackwell, Oxford.

Miller, D. 2008, *The Comfort of Things*. Polity, Malden, MA.

Miller, D. 2010, *Stuff*. Polity Press, Cambridge.

Miller, G. 1986, Of Fish or Sherds: A Model for Estimating Vessel Populations from Minimum Vessel Counts. *Historical Archaeology*, 20: 59–85.

Mitchell, S. 2009, *Daily Life in Victorian England*, Second Edition. Greenwood Press, London.

Mrozowski, S.A. 2006, *The Archaeology of Class in Urban America*. Cambridge University Press, Cambridge.

Murray, T. 2006, Integrating Archaeology and History at the "Commonwealth Block": "Little Lon" and Casselden Place. *International Journal of Historical Archaeology*, 10(4): 395–413.

Murray, T. 2011, Poverty in the Modern City: Retrospects and Prospects. *International Journal of Historical Archaeology*, 15(4): 572–581.

Murray, T. and A. Mayne 2001, Imaginary Landscapes: Reading Melbourne's "Little Lon". In A. Mayne and T. Murray (eds.) *The Archaeology of Urban Landscapes: Explorations in Slumland*, New Directions in Archaeology Series, University of Cambridge, Cambridge, pp. 89–105.

Nigel Lewis and Associates 1982, Former Smith Residence, 300 Queen Street, Melbourne: A Report on Its Architectural and Historical Significance. Report to the Department of Housing and Construction Victoria/Tasmania Region, Melbourne.

Orser Jr., C.E. 1994, Consumption, Consumerism, and Things from the Earth. *Historical Methods*, Spring 1994, 27(2): 61–70.

Parker, R. 1984, *The Subversive Stitch: Embroidery and the Making of the Feminine*. Women's Press, London.

Porter, J. and A. Ferrier 2004, Miscellaneous Artefacts. Unpublished report to the ISPT and Heritage Victoria, Melbourne.

Praetzellis, A. and M. Praetzellis 1992, Faces and Facades: Victorian Ideology in Early Sacramento. In A.E. Yentsch and M.C. Beaudry (eds.) *The Art and Mystery of Historical Archaeology: Essays in Honor of James Deetz*, CRC Press, Florida, pp. 75–99.

Praetzellis, A. and M. Praetzellis 2001, Mangling Symbols of Gentility in the Wild West: Case Studies in Interpretive Archaeology. *American Anthropologist*, 103(3): 645–654.

Praetzellis, A., M. Praetzellis and M.R. Brown III 1988, What Happened to the Silent Majority? Research Strategies for Studying Dominant Group Material Culture in Late Nineteenth-Century California. In M. Beaudry (ed.) *Documentary Archaeology in the New World*, Cambridge University Press, Cambridge, pp. 192–202.

Priestley, S. 1984, *The Victorians: Making Their Mark*. Fairfax, Syme & Weldon Associates, Sydney.

Prossor, L., S. Lawrence, A. Brooks and J. Lennon 2012, Household Archaeology, Lifecycles and Status in a Nineteenth-Century Australian Coastal Community. *International Journal of Historical Archaeology*, 16(4): 809–827.

Quirk, K. 2008a, The Colonial Goldfields: Visions and Revisions. *Australasian Historical Archaeology*, 26: 13–20.

Quirk, K. 2008b, The Victorians in "Paradise": Gentility as Social Strategy in the Archaeology of Colonial Australia. Unpublished PhD thesis, University of Queensland, Brisbane.

Rodriguez, A.C. and A. Brooks 2012, Speaking in Spanish, Eating in English; Ideology and Meaning in Nineteenth-Century British Transfer Prints in Barcelona, Anzoategui State, Venezuela. *Historical Archaeology*, 46(3): 47–62.

Rotman, D. 2009, *Historical Archaeology of Gendered Lives*. Contributions to Global Historical Archaeology, Springer, New York.

Russell, P. 1993, In Search of Woman's Place: An Historical Survey of Gender and Space in Nineteenth-Century Australia. *Australasian Historical Archaeology*, 11: 28–32.

Russell, P. 1994a, *For Richer, For Poorer: Early Colonial Marriages*. Melbourne University Press, Melbourne.

Russell, P. 1994b, *"A Wish of Distinction": Colonial Gentility and Femininity*. Melbourne University Press, Melbourne.

Russell, P. 2002, The Brash Colonial: Class and Comportment in Nineteenth-Century Australia. *Transactions of the Royal Historical Society*, 12: 431–453.

Russell, P. 2003, Cultures of Distinction. In H.-M. Teo and R. White (eds.) *Cultural History in Australia*, University of New South Wales Press, Sydney, pp. 158–260.

Russell, P. 2010, *Savage or Civilised? Manners in Colonial Australia*. New South, Sydney.

Samson, R. 1990, *The Social Archaeology of Houses*. Edinburgh University Press, Edinburgh.

Sato, N. and S. Hayes in prep, Gentility and Respectability: An Historical Archaeological Analysis of the 19th-Century Australian Middle Class.

Saunders, K. and R. Evans (eds.) 1992, *Gender Relations in Australia: Domination and Negotiation*. Harcourt Brace Jovanovich, Sydney.

Schiffer, M.B. 1987, *Formation Processes of the Archaeological Record*. University of New Mexico Press, Albuquerque.

Scott-Virtue, L. 1984a, 300 Queen Street Archaeological Report: Part I, Summary Report on the Archaeological Investigation. Report to the the Department of Housing and Construction, Melbourne.

Scott-Virtue, L. 1984b, 300 Queen Street Archaeological Report: Part II, Detailed Report on the Site Investigations and Excavations. Report to the the Department of Housing and Construction, Melbourne.

Serle, G. 1963, *The Golden Age: A History of the Colony of Victoria, 1851–1861*. Melbourne University Press, Melbourne.

Serle, G. 1971, *The Rush to Be Rich: A History of the Colony of Victoria, 1883–1889*. Melbourne University Press, Melbourne.

Shackel, P.A. 1993, *Personal Discipline and Material Culture: An Archaeology of Annapolis, Maryland 1796–1870*. The University of Tennessee Press, Knoxville.

Shackel, P.A. 2000, Craft to Wage Labor: Agency and Resistance in American Historical Archaeology. In M.-A. Dobres and J. E. Robb (eds.) *Agency in Archaeology*, Routledge, New York, pp. 232–246.

Shackel, P.A. 2010, Identity and Collective Action in a Multiracial Community. *Historical Archaeology*, 44(1): 58–71.

Shaw, A.G.L. 1996, *A History of the Port Phillip District: Victoria Before Separation*. Melbourne University Press, Melbourne.

Skeggs, B. 1997, *Formations of Class and Gender: Becoming Respectable*. Sage, London.

Smee, C.J. 1981, *The Pioneer Register: Containing Genealogical Details of Five Hundred Pioneers, Their Children & Grandchildren*. The 1788–1820 Association, Sydney.

Spencer-Wood, S. 1987, *Consumer Choice in Historical Archaeology*. Plenum Press, New York.

Spencer-Wood, S. 2013, *Historical and Archaeological Perspectives on Gender Transformations: From Private to Public*. Springer, New York.

Sprague, R. 2002, China or Prosser Button Identification and Dating. *Historical Archaeology*, 36(2): 111–127.

Sussman, L. 2000, Objects vs. Sherds: A Statistical Evaluation. In K. Karklins (ed.) *Studies in Material Culture Research*, Society for Historical Archaeology, California, Pennsylvania, pp. 96–103.

Swain, S. 2005, Social Mobility. In A. Brown-May and S. Swain (eds.) *The Encyclopedia of Melbourne*, Cambridge University Press, Melbourne, pp. 668–669.

Sykes, M. 1988, Lace Makers' Bobbins. *The Antique Collector*, National Magazine Co., London.

Symonds, J. 2003, An Imperial People? Highland Scots, Emigration and the British Colonial World. In S. Lawrence (ed.) *Archaeologies of the British: Explorations of Identity in Great Britain and its Colonies 1600–1945*, Routledge, London, pp. 138–155.

Thompson, E. 1994, *Fair Enough: Egalitarianism in Australia*. University of New South Wales Press, Sydney.

Vader, J. 1975, *Antique Bottle Collecting in Australia*. Summit Books, Sydney.

Walker, R. 1984, *Under Fire: A History of Tobacco*

Smoking in Australia. Melbourne University Press, Melbourne.

Wall, D.D. 1992, Sacred Dinners and Secular Teas: Constructing Domesticity in Mid-19th-Century New York. *Historical Archaeology*, 25: 69–81.

Wall, D.D. 1994, *The Archaeology of Gender: Separating the Spheres in Urban America*. Plenum Press, New York.

Webb, J., T. Schirato and G. Danaher 2002, *Understanding Bourdieu*. Allen & Unwin, Sydney.

Wilkie, L. 2000, Not Merely Child's Play: Creating a Historical Archaeology of Children and Childhood. In J. S. Derevenski (ed.) *Children and Material Culture*, Routledge, London, pp. 100–113.

Williams, P. 1978, *Staffordshire: Romantic Transfer Patterns*. Fountain House East, Jeffersontown.

Williamson, C. 2006, Dating the Domestic Ceramics and Pipe Smoking Related Artifacts from Casselden Place, Melbourne, Australia. *International Journal of Historical Archaeology*, 10(4): 329–341.

Woff, B. 2014, Bottle Reuse and Archaeology: Evidenced from the Site of a Bottle Merchant's Business. Unpublished Honours thesis, La Trobe University, Melbourne.

Woodhead, E.I., C. Sullivan and G. Gusset 1984, *Lighting Devices in the National Reference Collection, Parks Canada*. National Historic Parks and Sites Branch, Parks Canada, Ottawa.

Wurst, L. 2006, A Class All Its Own: Explorations of Class Formation and Conflict. In M. Hall and S.W. Silliman (eds.) *Historical Archaeology*, Blackwell, Malden, pp. 190–206.

Wurst, L. and R.K. Fitts 1999, Introduction: Why Confront Class?. *Historical Archaeology*, 33(1): 1–6.

Wurst, L. and R.H. McgGuire 1999, Immaculate Consumption: A Critique of the "Shop Till You Drop" School of Human Behaviour. *International Journal of Historical Archaeology*, 3(3): 191–199.

Yamin, R. 1998, Lurid Tales and Homely Stories of New York's Notorious Five Points. *Historical Archaeology*, 32(1): 74–85.

Yamin, R. 2002, Children's Strikes, Parents' Rights: Paterson and Five Points. *International Journal of Historical Archaeology*, 6(2): 113–126.

Yentsch, A. 1991, The Symbolic Divisions of Pottery: Sex-Related Attributes of English and Anglo-American Household Pots. In R.H. McGuire and R. Paynter (eds.) *The Archaeology of Inequality*, Blackwell, Oxford, pp. 192–230.

Young, L. 2003, *Middle-Class Culture in the Nineteenth Century: America, Australia and Britain*. Palgrave Macmillan, Hampshire.

Young, L. 2004, "Extensive, Economical and Elegant": The Habitus of Gentility in Early Nineteenth Century Sydney. *Australian Historical Studies*, 36(124): 201–220.

Young, L. 2010, Gentility: A Historical Context for the Material Culture of the Table in the "Long 19th Century". In J. Symonds (ed.) *Table Settings: The Material Culture and Social Context of Dining AD 1700–1900*, Oxbow, Oxford, pp. 133–143.

Index

Plates

Plate 1: Transfer-printed and hand-painted Chinoise pattern plate (HA1651 – note glaze run and other flaws).

Plate 2: Chinese flowers plate from matching set (HA1641).

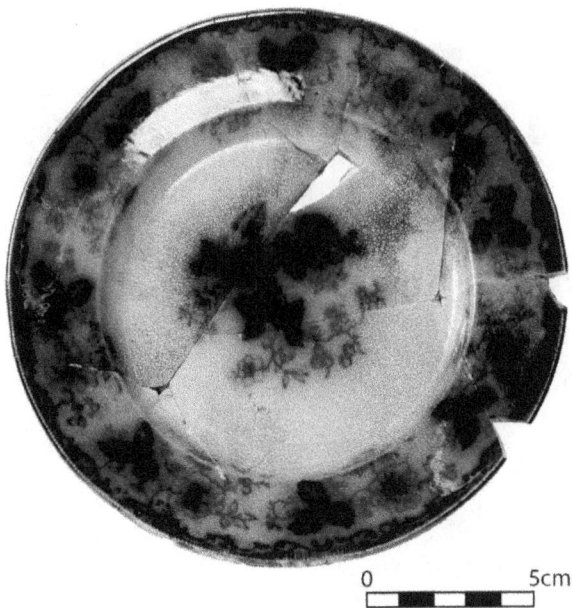

Plate 3: 'Alpine' pattern plate from matching set (HA1716.1).

Plate 4: 'Dagger Border' pattern plate (HA1649).

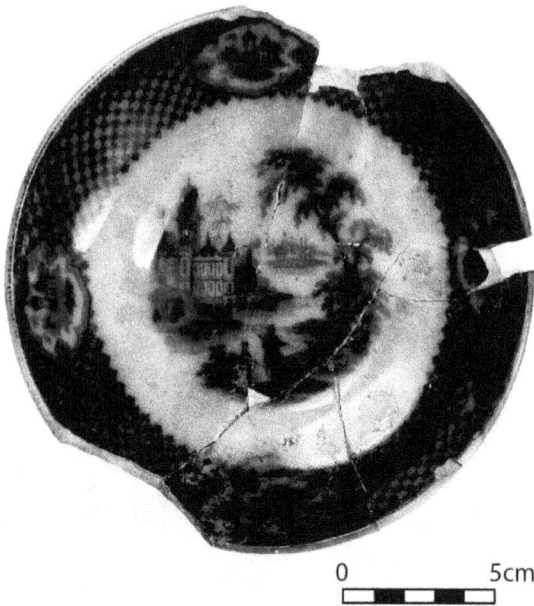

0   5cm

Plate 5: 'Cyrene' pattern saucer made by John and Thomas Lockett (HA1728).

0   3cm

Plate 6: Whiteware mustard jar (HA1655).

0   3cm

Plate 7: Bristol glazed stoneware bung jar (HA1570).

0   5cm

Plate 8: Transfer-printed chamber pot (HA1657).

www.ingramcontent.com/pod-product-compliance
Lightning Source LLC
Chambersburg PA
CBHW080841270326
41927CB00013B/3066

* 9 7 8 1 7 4 3 3 2 6 1 5 2 *